HOW TO MAKE MONEY WITH YOUR MICROCOMPUTER

No. 335
$14.95

HOW TO MAKE MONEY WITH YOUR MICROCOMPUTER

BY
CARL TOWNSEND & MERL MILLER

TAB BOOKS Inc.
BLUE RIDGE SUMMIT, PA. 17214

FIRST EDITION

FIRST PRINTING

Hardcover edition published in 1982 by TAB BOOKS inc.
Copyright © 1979 by Robotics Press

Printed in the United States of America

Townsend, Carl, 1938-
    How to make money with your microcomputer.

    Includes index.
    1. Small business—Handbooks, manuals, etc.   2. Computer
service industry.   3. Microcomputers.I. Miller, Merl K., 1942-
    I. Title.
HF5356.T74   1982   001.64   81-21398
ISBN 0-8306-4335-4   AACR2

To Sandy, for all her help

CWT

To my children, who always wanted
to see their names in a book:
  Patricia Abigail Miller
  Susan Wissler Miller
  Merl Kem Miller, Jr.

MKM

The authors gratefully acknowledge the help of Nels Winkless III, Jim Warren, Dick Heiser and Gib Springer in writing this book.

PREFACE

A few years ago it would have cost several man-years of your effort to earn enough to purchase even the smallest minicomputer system. Today you can purchase a microcomputer system for a few months of your income. This sytem is not a toy or application-bound to small jobs. It is fully capable of handling the accounting of a small business, laboratory reporting for a clinical laboratory, statistical analysis of the stock market or planning your investment strategy.

This microcomputer system can be used as a "lever" to multiply your income, and it is a tool of great power. It can do many jobs the individual cannot do at all and can process routine jobs in much less time than it would take you to do them by hand. The possibilities are limited only by your imagination and creativity. This book will give you a start with dozens of proven money-making ideas.

Perhaps you already have a few ideas in mind but so far haven't been able to integrate the ideas into a profitable income-returning project. You'll find this book will help you to make those ideas work for you.

If the system prices still seem too high, don't give up those ideas. Lease a system for three months from a friend or buy a little computer time and make those ideas work! Soon you'll have the money for the whole system, as well as the experience of making the computer work for you!

CONTENTS

1 HOW TO WRITE ARTICLES

1.1 HOW TO FIND A MARKET

Your first task is to identify a market, some publisher or reader who will pay you money for the opportunity to publish or read your work. The point here is to make money using your specific knowledge of microcomputers. This involves not merely writing articles, but selling them. Good ideas for articles are a dime a dozen; good ideas that have been carefully tailored for a particular audience are hard to find. Editors search for such materials diligently, and they pay hard cash willingly when they find articles of value to their readers.

There is a wide variety of magazines that publish articles on microcomputer subjects (Appendix B). Some of these are high quality publications that attract professional writers, while others seem to have difficulty finding enough good articles to fill their pages. Most micocomputer magazines fall somewhere in between. None of these magazines (such as *Interface Age, Byte, Creative Computing,* and *Kilobaud*) has been in existence long enough to acquire a wide reputation, however, they all publish good material.

As there is already a critical need for more high-quality specialty publications, you may choose to publish a newsletter yourself or write articles for existing magazines. Some of these periodicals are evolving to meet new needs, as in the case of *Interface Age*, which is attempting to reach the business community. Other application areas are hurting for good writers, advertising, and application information. These areas could be addressed by smaller newsletters easily published by individuals or small application communities (see *How To Make $25,000 a Year Publishing Newsletters*, by Brian Sheehan, Parker Publications Co., Inc., 1971). Good examples of such publications would be newsletters for community networking, special games (such as Star Trek or chess), control applications, teleconferencing or business application areas (as word processing). Some of these newsletters already exist at various levels of quality.

Another type of support periodical is the user group publication. Many of these groups (Alpha Micro, Technico, Heath, CP/M) now exist as organizations. The problem is that the projected computer growth in the next few years is forecasted at several orders of magnitude. Amateur support groups will not be able to handle this volume, and most groups will need to become more professional and fulltime in much the same manner as other organizations. For example, the professional ARRL organization represents amateur radio operators. All this means obtaining qualified fulltime professional support and producing more publications to keep everyone informed of what is happening. It also means there will be a large market for "amateur" article writers.

While you may be able to sell an article to a general market magazine, you will probably have better luck selling your article if you start with a "microcomputer" magazine. In these magazines you will find monthly serial articles on TTL logic, artificial intelligence and business applications. These magazines buy complex accounting programs, word processing software, and robot construction articles. They also buy one-page articles on neon flashers, simple games and strange science fiction. What would you like to write about? You can probably get it published if you follow a few simple quidelines.

Let's start with the basics. What should you write about? Well, what do you know? You may be saying to yourself, "Not much." Okay, but what were you just explaining to your friend in the computer club? Was it a chess program, a method of soldering without burning your fingers, or a method of converting octal to binary, or . . . ? Any of these ideas can be turned into a useful, informative article for a particular audience.

If you are writing a book, publish a chapter as a article and let an appropriate magazine know about the book. If you are developing a product, write an article on why the market needs your product; or explain someone else's product. If you are developing some software, publish a simplified version of the package (*not* a preliminary version—it should be debugged!).

You can find plenty of opportunities for articles. If your community produces an amateur computer show, write an article on how it was done (use plenty of pictures). If you have an interesting computer personality in your area, interview him or her with some good questions you have always wanted to ask. *Personal Computing* magazine has some excellent examples of this type of article.

Magazines generally target their articles for a specific readership. Typical readership classifications include:

The prehobbyist
The hobbyist
The advanced hobbyist
The computer retailer
The manufacturer
The businessman
The computer professional (hardware and systems)
The computer professional (software)
The professional educator

Identify the markets addressed by the magazines you wish to write for and direct your message to the specific readership of the magazine.

Magazines also vary in the types of articles they publish. If you plan a construction article, you will not want to send it to *Dr. Dobbs*, as this publication prefers software articles and product reviews. Study the magazines and see how they differ. Identify the types of articles they publish, which may include:

Software and programs (assembly level)
Software (BASIC-type programs)
Science fiction
Construction
Philosophy
Tutorial—software
Tutorial—hardware
Systems analysis
Product review (software and hardware)
Applications
Humor

What type of article do you plan to write?

Study the magazines you receive. What types of articles would you like to see? What did the authors omit? What ideas can be expanded? Can it be rewritten at a different technical level? Keep a list of all your ideas. Check *The Periodical Guide for Computers* (E. Berg Publications, 1360 S.W. 199th Ct., Aloha, Oregon 97005) to see if the idea has been previously pursued. Remember that the magazine editor will be receiving hundreds of manuscripts; why should he read yours? The magazine readers will read many magazines; why should they read your article? Write something that will help the editor fill the pages with material which rewards the readers for making the effort to read it.

1.2 HOW TO WRITE YOUR ARTICLE

Once you have your idea, you are ready to start writing. Try to follow these 12 steps:

1. Make a list of topics and ideas. Jot down everything that comes to mind, do not worry about order.
2. Write a rough outline. Sort your topics and ideas into some kind of order.
3. Write a good outline. Now try to put your topics and ideas into a usable form, paying particular attention to details. Throw out topics that do not apply and add new ones.
4. Write a rough draft. Before you start on the rough draft, do two things: Read your outline carefully, then put it away. Try to write your draft in large sections, referring only occasionally to your outline or notes. Just let it flow—you will be surprised at how easily it goes.
5. Revise the rough draft. Now you can refer to your outline and notes. Carefully go through your draft, adding comments, correcting grammar and spelling, and deleting superfluous material. Edit and correct all technical material.
6. Write the second draft, starting with the first word of the first sentence, and rewriting the entire article. You can refer to the rough draft when necessary.
7. Do a line-by-line revision of the second draft. Consider each sentence alone. Can it be improved? How? Is the sentence really necessary? Does it lead logically into the next sentence?

8. Write the final draft. Do a total rewrite of the second draft and type it.
9. Edit and revise the final draft.
10. Do a line-by-line revision of the final draft.
11. An effective way to proof is to read it in "sentence reverse" order. Read the last sentence of the article first, second to last sentence next, and so on.
12. Retype, if necessary; insert photos, drawings, and print-outs. Submit the article.

This process will save you a lot of headaches, especially Step 3; you must have an outline. Why? Mainly, because it helps consolidate your thinking. Every article should have a structural design that allows you to emphasize your most important points and to relate these points to one another. It also has a beginning, middle and end. The middle is further divided into a number of separate sections so carefully put together that each paragraph fits into only one place. There are no alternative locations for it. You can make sure this happens by creating and following an outline.

Now that you are convinced that writing an outline is necessary, where do you start? Begin by keeping in mind that the outline is for your benefit only; usually no one else is going to read it. Every item on your outline should be a key that triggers creative thought. Use key words, phrases or sentences, but make it meaningful. Make little notes to yourself where appropriate. For instance, you may have the key word "program." Next to it you might write, "use assembly language—explain why."

If the purpose of writing an outline is to give your article a basic structure, it follows that your outline should have a structure. This one works:

I. Main idea
   A. Key subject
      1. Topic
      2. Topic
   B. Key subject
II. Main idea

The advantage of using this kind of outline is that it shows you exactly where you are going. Here is a sample outline:

I. Basics of article writing
   A. 12 steps

   B. What we are going to do
      1. Outline
      2. Drafts
      3. Thoughts about writing
      4. Reference sources
II. Outlines
   A. Purpose
      1. Consolidate thinking
      2. Logical organization of thought
   B. Some basic principles
      1. The key that triggers thought
      2. Structure and style
   C. Outline of this column
III. Importance of drafts
   A. Why more than one
   B. Editing and revising (reference sources)
IV. Some thoughts about writing
   A. Putting it together
      1. Logical organization of thought
      2. Clarity is the primary goal
      3. Things to do
         a. Specific detail
         b. Examples
         c. Drawings or photos
   B. Sentences
      1. Short, clear, well constructed
      2. Single ideas
   C. Say what you have to say in clearest possible manner
      1. When cogitating . . .
      2. Other words, keep it simple (KISS)
   D. The reader
      1. Know the reader
      2. Keep the reader in mind
      3. Inform the reader
V.   Reference sources
   A. Dictionary
   B. Thesaurus
   C. Look it up
   D. Sippl/Kidd

Once you have a good outline, you are ready to start your rough draft. You can either keep your outline on hand for reference, or read it and set it aside. Try both. No matter how you use the outline, it should serve as the structure for your rough draft.

Your rough draft will be exactly that—rough! Don't try to correct things as you go; just put your thoughts on paper. Go entirely through a draft before you attempt to edit or revise it. This is time consuming and cumbersome, but it is worth it. Follow a set pattern, your work should hang together. This leads us to the most important part of revising: be vicious. Cut out everything that is not clear, concise, and necessary.

Clarity is the primary goal of good writing, so try to organize your thoughts in a logical manner. This can best be done by remembering:

1. Follow your outline
2. Explain things carefully
3. Give examples
4. Be specific
5. Remember your reader
6. Include drawings, photographs, or programs to amplify your comments
7. Write short, clear, well-constructed sentences
8. Restrict each sentence to a single thought

Most important, when cogitating about indicating a treatise, one is obliged to pursue an elementary prescript: eschew obfuscation. In other words, keep it simple. Always keep your reader in mind. Remember, your purpose is to inform or educate your reader, so write to him in the same way you would talk to a friend.

Consider reference sources. Obviously you need technical sources, but you should also have a few language sources to aid you in literary works. Two books are especially helpful: The thesaurus will give you words you can use, such as synonyms. For instance, suppose you want to use the word "program," but you do not want to refer to a "computer program." The thesaurus will give you these alternatives: agendum, procedure (plan), schedule, bulletin, calendar (list).

As your thesaurus will give you words, *Look It Up* will give you ideas and usage. Examples:

compute—do not use "compute" when "figure" will do
moo, mooed, mooing
program, programmed/programed, programmer/programer, programming/programing
debug—listed as standard usage in *Webster's*

The books listed below are generally available at most book-stores:

Roget's New Pocket Thesaurus in Dictionary Form, by Lewis (Pocket Books)

Look It Up, by Rudolf Flesch (Harper and Row)

Webster's New World Dictionary of the American Language (Prentice-Hall)

Microcomputer Dictionary and Guide, by Charles J. Sippl and David A. Kidd (Matrix Publishers, Inc.)

1.3 "HOW TO" ARTICLES

Most personal computing articles are of the "how to" type. There are some fundamental rules to follow when writing the how-to article. The most important: your directions must be absolutely clear and must work for anyone, anywhere. The following instructions may not be applicable to every situation, but it is a good idea to use them whenever possible:

First Paragraph: Name your subject immediately and give your reader some reasons for wanting to continue reading your article. Follow this with a list of reasons for doing the job your way: economy, speed, ease for the novice, whatever.

Second Paragraph: Make a list of everything your reader will need to complete the project, run the programs, etc. If you are assuming some fundamental knowledge (for instance, programming ability in BASIC), provide some reference sources. If special equipment or tools are required, give their approximate costs.

Third Paragraph and Beyond: Starting with the first step, explain all the procedures involved. Use the present tense and end on a high point. A good ending is as important as a good opening. Re-emphasize the highlights of your article.

1.4 HOW TO SUBMIT YOUR ARTICLE

There are a few conventions you should observe. First, your manuscript should be typed, doublespaced, on a good white paper. It should be at least three typewritten pages. Put your full name and address in the upper left corner of the first page, and your last name, title of the article, and page number in the upper left corner of succeeding pages. If part of your article contains copyrighted material, you must obtain permission from the copyright holder in order to use it. The permission given is for worldwide rights to the first printing and all reprints.

Line drawings and other artwork present special problems for the magazine. Line drawings are generally redone, so they need not be in final form—just understandable. If you cannot draw, supply a written description with the drawings: "Dear Magazine Artist, The funny-looking box with dots in it is a microcomputer; the wiggly lines are fingers." Photographs should be included if at all possible. The best photos, of course, are 8″×10″ glossies. Make sure everything is clear and focused. A simple test is to hold the photo at arm's length and look at it carefully. This test works even better with computer printouts. If the printout can be read from a distance of a couple feet, it will probably produce in the magazine. Printouts are reproduced from the original, so be sure to send a good copy. Use a high-quality white paper and a new ribbon.

The price paid by a magazine for an article varies widely. *Interface Age* pays $15 to $50 a page, plus an additional $15 a page for software. *Kilobaud* pays $100 to $300 per article. A good series of articles can pay you well over $1,000. There are other magazines which pay little or nothing for articles.

To find whether your subject is attractive to a magazine, you may query the magazine before you write the article. For example:

Mr. Wayne Green, Publisher
Kilobaud
1001001, Inc.
Peterborough, NH 03458
Dear Mr. Green:
Would your readers be interested in a short article explaining how to develop a mailing list? I project an article of about three pages* that would give the listings for the program and show how to implement it.
I look forward to hearing from you.

Sincerely,

Carl Townsend
4110 N. E. Alameda
Portland, OR 97212

* Note that a page of solid text in a conventional magazine contains 900 to 1000 words. A typewritten page of manuscript contains about 250 words. (Do not crowd the page, the editor needs space to scribble.)

If you have already written the article, do not query—send the article.

Magazine articles offer rewards beyond the cash they bring: they will give you and your organization professional credibility. If you plan to earn your way professionally in the microcomputer business, you should occasionally write and publish. Your article may be rewritten by professional writers, but it will still carry your name and add to your professional image. This image will help you sell your professional services.

1.5 MAKING MONEY FROM BOOK REVIEWS

Book reviewing is an easy way to add to your income. It is, however, a skill that must be learned. The best way to get recognition as a book reviewer is to submit some reviews to your favorite magazine. Magazines are always interested in reviews and will publish most they receive.

Generally, you will get one of two responses. Either the editor will publish your review, or he will tell you why it is unacceptable. If he publishes it, you are "in." He will probably send you additional books to review. Initially, there will be no fee other than a free copy of the book you are reviewing. Once you establish yourself, however, you will normally be paid a fee equal to the magazine's usual rates.

The primary reasons your review might not be acceptable are poor writing and unfairness. Good writing is a matter of practice, so let us turn our attention to unfairness.

Every book written has faults. Regardless of how careful an author is, mistakes will be made and some people will be offended. If you are going to be a good reviewer, you must accept the fact that there are going to be problems. Once you learn to assess these problems in context and offer constructive criticism about them, you will be acceptable as a reviewer. On the other hand, it is not a good idea to praise everything. The key to writing a good review is to make an honest appraisal of the book, without bias. If you do not like a particular author or publishers, do not review their books. Remember that your purpose is to aid the prospective reader of the book, not to reform the author's character.

Once you establish yourself as a fair reviewer, you will be in a position to review books not only for magazines, but for book publishers. Any good publisher will welcome reviews by an unbiased outside source before publishing the book.

Most books go through a fairly complicated review process prior to publication. The manuscript is reviewed before it is accepted, during actual preparation, and right before it is released for production. Usually two or three reviewers examine the manuscript at each stage. As a general rule, a publisher will reject 50 to 75 percent of all manuscripts submitted. This means that each published book represents a dozen or so reviews, all of which are paid. Fees run from $50 to $250 or more, depending on the complexity of the review and the ability of the reviewer. It is something you can do—all it takes is some writing ability, a good grasp of your subject, and a lot of practice.

Your special knowledge of microcomputers gives you an opportunity to make money from publishers in a number of ways.

1.6 USING THE COMPUTER TO PROCESS THE ARTICLE

Your microcomputer system can be used as a word processor to set up, edit, and print your article. As an example, we recently used our system to set up a speech (and an eventual article) for the Third West Coast Computer Faire. The article was typed directly from our computer to a two-column special form they required for article submission. The four-page article took six hours to process. More details on this follow in the next chapter.

2 HOW TO GET YOUR MICROCOMPUTER BOOK PUBLISHED

In this chapter we will cover the writing and selling of a book. Let's start with selling it—if you can't sell it, there's no reason to write it.

With the increasing market for microcomputers, there is a sharply increasing market for books on the subject. The reason is simple: books are inexpensive when compared with systems. For every person who owns a system there are several others who would like to, and all these people are potential customers for your book. People who have systems also buy books, they are anxious to know how their system works and how to write software.

There are two ways to publish your book: do it yourself, or have someone else publish it for you. We feel that the best way is to have it published by someone else. There are a lot of reasons why we feel this way, but probably the best one is that you'll make more money.

2.1 PUBLISH IT YOURSELF

The primary disadvantages of publishing the book yourself are time, labor and money. Unless you have a lot of capital to invest, and a reasonable amount of luck, you probably won't profit. Look at it this way: if you spend 20 hours a week marketing your book and make $5,000 from the book, you are working for $5 an hour. In addition, you are getting a $0 return on your investment. Of course, there are examples of people who have been successful, but the odds are really against you. If you want to be a book publisher, be one. If you want to be a computerist or a writer, don't try to be a publisher.

Now that we have told you all the reasons not to publish the book yourself, it seems only fair that we tell you how to do it yourself. If you have the capital and the time, you just might be one of the fortunate few.

Let's start with a simple book that won't cost you very much. Begin by drawing all the figures with India ink. Make each figure about one-third of an 8½″×11″ page. Next, carefully type the manuscript, using a carbon ribbon. If you use a word processing system with your typewriter, you should be able to produce near-perfect typing. Be sure to leave space for the figures, which should be pasted into the manuscript using clear tape, a glue stick, or rubber cement. Have the book printed by a local quick-copy printer and have him spiral bind the book with plastic covers.

Here are two manufacturers from which you can get plastic covers:

General Binding Corporation
Northbrook, IL 60062

Inter Binding Company
15955 W. 5th Avenue
Golden, CO 80401

Here are printing and binding expenses for a typical book:

Printing: 200 pages @ 2¢ per page	$4.00
Binding	1.50
	$5.50

You should charge about $11 for this book, which will allow you a reasonable profit and some expense money for marketing. If you sell through computer stores you may want to set your price a little higher, as these stores will expect a 40 percent discount. Initially, though, you will probably want to sell this book directly to the customers. You can best do this by using someone else's mailing list. Figure your cost at about 25 cents per name. You should get about a 2-3 percent return. Remember, however, the more books you create, the more time you will have to spend printing, marketing, and delivering books. (At some point in time, you may well begin to wonder if it's worth it.)

2.2 HOW AND WHAT TO SUBMIT TO A BOOK PUBLISHER

Before we discuss the writing of a book, let's look at how to sell the manuscript to a publisher. The first thing to consider is what to submit for a review and how to submit it.

A publisher will always consider the complete manuscript, but a publishing decision can be made on the basis of a detailed outline, two or three representative chapters and a prospectus. This is sufficient because it gives the reviewer a good grasp of the material and allows him to evaluate the author's style, pedagogy and technical competence. The publisher may have from one to ten or more reviewers comment on the material, but the norm is two or three reviewers.

The publisher will decide to do one of three things: publish the book, reject the book, or send it back for revision. Let's look at all three of these alternatives separately.

If the publisher wants to publish the book, how do you decide whether you want to publish with that house? Publishers' royalty schedules, book production capabilities and marketing abilities vary greatly. Royalites are normally paid on net proceeds from sales of the book. Net proceeds constitute actual monies the publisher receives or is due to receive from accounts receivable. The royalty scale varies from a low of 5 percent to a high of 25 percent. Marketing ability is something you will have to judge for yourself. One good criterion is to start with publishers with whom you are most familiar. Be sure you are dealing with legitimate publishers, not someone who publishes books as a sideline. Remember, there is more to publishing a book than just printing what the author submits.

Now, for the other two alternatives. If your book is rejected, find out why. Revise it as necessary and submit it to another publisher.

If the publisher returns the book for revision, try to make all the suggested revisions and add something. You should be able to tell from the publisher's comments what the reviewer does and does not like about your manuscript. Change what he doesn't like and add some more of what he does like.

As for the physical preparation of samples, it is best to prepare three copies; submit two copies and keep one. It should be typed (doublespaced) and should include any charts, graphs and photographs you feel are pertinent. However, the material does not have to be in perfect form. The emphasis in preparing material should be on readability.

Consider the samples: representative chapters, detailed outline, and prospectus. You should pick two or three chapters which you consider to be an integral part of the book. They should be in the best possible form but do not have to follow a specific order. For instance, you could submit chapters One, Three and Six of an eight-chapter book, as long as you feel that these chapters represent what you are trying to do and that they put your writing style and pedagogy in the best possible light. It is a good idea to submit any chapter which you feel is particularly innovative or unique. You should, however, include chapter One. If a customer in a bookstore or computer store picks up your book, he will probably glance through chapter One. Chapter One may determine whether or not the book sells, so the publisher is keenly interested in this chapter.

The detailed outline should encompass the entire book, including the chapters being submitted. This gives the reviewer an idea of how the remaining chapters are going to be developed. It should include chapter headings, subheadings, sub-subheadings and explanations of each, as necessary. If possible, it should be in this form:

Title of Book
 I. Chapter Title
   A. First subject
     1. First topic
       Sentence description of topic
   B. Second subject
     1. First topic
       Sentence description of topic
 II. Chapter Title
   A. First subject
     1. First topic
       Sentence description of topic

The prospectus, simply stated, is an abstract of the book with market considerations. You should say for whom the book is intended and why. It is insufficient to say that it is intended for computer hobbyists, for example. You should point out what background you expect your readers to have; for instance, you could say, "This book assumes that the reader has a fundamental background in microcomputers such as that provided in Didday's *Home Computers: 2^{10} Questions and Answers, Volumes 1 and 2*." You should look at the existing books and compare yours to them. Discuss specifically what their weaknesses and strengths are and spell out why your book is better. If your book competes with, say, half of another book, it is a good idea to mention that book anyway, so the reviewer and publisher have some basis on which to compare your materials. This is particularly true if you are writing a book in an area where there are no books. The prospectus should be written for the reviewer but, if at all possible, at a level the editor (who usually has little technical background) can understand. Last, and probably most important, ask yourself, "Given the detailed outline and representative chapters, what else can I say to the reviewer to put my book in the best possible light?"

Once you have your manuscript in hand, you are ready to contact publishers. You can find most publishers' addresses in the *Literary Market Place*. This book is available in the reference section of your library. See the Appendix for a list of additional publishers.

2.3 GUIDELINES FOR WRITING YOUR BOOK

Creating a book is not a mysterious act known only to the initiated. It is the process of logically presenting a systemized body of knowledge in a manner suitable to the intended audience. The most important thing to remember is to *identify the needs of your reader*.

You already know what you want to say—you want to tell someone else about your favorite subject. Who this "someone else" is will, to a large extent, determine how you go about presenting your information.

Readers generally develop a fairly good notion of the author's attitude toward them. If your reader thinks you are being patronizing or ignoring legitimate questions, he will become either bored or irritated and quit reading your book. You can avoid this by always keeping your audience in mind as you write. One good way is to *write out* a thorough description of the audience you want to reach.

You can make your audience come to life by visualizing one person who has all the important characteristics of the audience. This can be someone you know, a composite of several people or someone you fabricate. Call him "Joe" and take his point of view every once in a while. You will find that he will help control the whole writing process.

Once you have your audience in mind, you will want to define your goals for writing the book. Try to see your book from the reader's viewpoint—what can you say that will get and hold his interest? What topics should be covered? In what detail?

What type of book should you write? Here are some suggestions:

Type of Book	Sample
"How-To"	instruction manual for computers, construction manual for interfaces
Tutorial	how computers work, software (i.e., BASIC in this book)
Survey Manual	survey of equipment or software
Software	canned programs, game collections, business applications
Humor	cartoons, stories
Social Impact	philosophy, futuristic

Regardless of what you decide to write about, write out a plan. By setting down *in writing* exactly what you hope to accomplish, you will keep your focus sharp and control the natural impulse to digress.

You now have two documents which you should have on hand during the entire writing process. But if you find that they are shoving your thoughts in a direction that is increasingly uncomfortable, it is time to stop and re-think your approach. You may have made a mistake in your analysis. Instead of putting your ideas into a framework that won't work, go back to the beginning; re-define your audience and goals. This may seem painfully time-consuming, but you will find, in the long run, that you will save a lot of time and distress.

Now you have the vital orientation to control your presentation. You know your audience and what you want to accomplish with them. You have a working idea of the preconceptions, prejudices and gaps in knowledge they are likely to have, as well as their strengths.

Once you have your orientation, you are ready to work out the basic logic and organization of your approach. Start by writing a one-paragraph summary of your book. In every subject there is a natural logic inherent in the relationship between its components. The best way to uncover this natural logic is to condense it into a single paragraph. If you prepare your summary paragraph carefully, the components of your idea and their relative importance will fall into place.

This summary can serve as the foundation for dividing your subject into its basic parts, each of which will constitute a chapter in your work.

The first step in this process is to decide on a device or method of organization. How you choose to break down your subject is a matter of personal preference. The important point is that you settle on a plan which suits your subject matter and approach, then stick to it.

Special care must be taken to assure that the divisions of your subject are of roughly the same importance. These divisions will ultimately be chapters. If your book is to be balanced and in proportion, you must establish divisions that accurately identify the components of your subject. These divisions should also give you enough scope to develop the ideas contained in each.

Now you're ready to do for each chapter what you did for the book as a whole. This must be an orderly process, so you should follow these steps:

1. Write each chapter summary, being careful to state exactly what information will be included.
2. Look at the order of the chapters. Have you put any carts before their horses? Does the material develop by building naturally on the information in the preceding chapter and prepare for what follows?
3. Review your work regularly. Is the order of the chapters the most compelling possible? Does each unit contain only material relevant to itself? If not, now is the time to reorganize.

As you work, ideas will occur to you which apply to a different section. Resist the temptation to make these ideas somehow fit. Instead, jot them next to the chapter summary for which they are appropriate and include them in the development of that chapter.

You should now be free of the problem of logic and organization. You are ready, at long last, to turn your energies to casting your ideas in graceful, clear language—again with your audience uppermost in your mind.

Although you will want to avoid jargon as much as possible, you will still probably need to develop a small vocabulary of special terms. You do not have to use a dictionary to define terms; in fact, it is better if you don't. Dictionary definitions tend to be long and tedious, whereas you will be using terms only in a limited context. Be sure to think of your audience when defining terms. Can "Joe" understand what you mean?

Nothing brings an idea to light as well as a carefully chosen metaphor. For instance, in discussing organization we might have described your idea as a pile of bricks. A pile of bricks is just a pile of bricks until a bricklayer places them in order; then they become a designed structure. Your system of organization is the framework which turns your ideas from a random group of thoughts into an orderly structure.

As you write, you will also want to establish a "tone." Do you want to be informal with your reader? Or do you want to come across more authoritatively—more formally? Do you like to use words playfully or would you prefer to remain unobstrusive and let the information speak for itself?

This is, of course, a matter for your discretion, but it is important to be consistent. If you are chatty and full of anecdotes in Chapter One, it will confuse your reader if he finds you suddenly authoritative and assertive in Chapter Two and then switching tones again in Chapter Three. Remember that your logic and organization will win the confidence and respect of your reader. Your diction and rhetoric will win his good will.

2.4 ELEMENTS OF STYLE

How long should your book be? How extensive should it be? One way to answer these questions is to make a comparison between article writing and book writing. The obvious difference is length. An article might be 1,000 to 2,500 words long, while a book will be 50,000 to 150,000 words or more. The average microcomputer book is about 80,000 words, or 40 times the length of an article. However, you can't just put 40 articles together; a book must have a central idea or theme.

In deciding how long a book should be, there is, on one hand, the problem of reader resistance and, on the other hand, the desire to cover the subject completely. The primary causes of excessive manuscript length are lack of self-control and wordiness. Often the original plan is a good one, but the author goes off on tangents. You can avoid this by staying with your plan. Be sure you have a carefully written-out plan as described in Section 2.3. Refer to your plan and detailed outline frequently. Revise them when necessary, checking each chapter against the outline, and plan as you write.

Wordiness is more difficult to correct because it is more insidious; it is a reflection of a mental habit. Certainly it takes willpower and deliberate effort to think through each sentence as you write it. Strip away all the words that add nothing to the meaning of the sentence. Reject the several approximate words that come easily to mind and select the exact word. Make direct statements that inform rather than impress your reader. Avoid needless words or ideas. (For instance, don't say "visible to the eye" when "visible" will suffice.) Express simple ideas in simple language. Above all, recognize that hazy expressions are the result of hazy thinking. Clarify or reject each thought. This method of writing is tedious but will produce the best results.

Be brief but, in being brief, don't be obscure. Write as simply as the subject allows, using words from the general vocabulary whenever you can without sacrificing accuracy. Most important, write to inform.

2.5 HOW TO USE YOUR COMPUTER TO PUT YOUR BOOK TOGETHER

A microcomputer system can be used as an excellent word processor if you have the right type of system. The printer should print both upper and lower case with crisp, clear copies. The ideal printers are the daisy wheel printers that type at about 45 to 55 characters per second. High-speed dot matrix printers are not suitable for manuscript processing. If your budget is small, purchase a heavy-duty used Selectric with a parallel or serial interface. One word of caution: IBM makes two types of Selectric mechanisms. The inexpensive type is used in office machines and typewriters for normal office use. They also make another heavy-duty mechanism with better bearings and components for computer interfacing. These heavy-duty mechanisms sold in printers for thousands of dollars a few years ago, but can now be purchased used for about $300 to $500, depending on their condition. Properly interfaced, these machines should average about two service calls a year under very heavy use. Typing speed is one-third that of a daisy wheel printer, or 15 characters a second.

Cassette storage can be used for your text, but a mini- or full-sized disk system is better. Cassettes are slow, time consuming, have poor reliability, and are difficult to index and file. Disks are worth the extra cost if you can afford them. A mini-disk costs 70 percent of the cost of a full-sized disk but can store only 40 percent as much data. It is also slower than a full-sized disk.

The video terminal should have 24 lines of 80 characters each, with both upper and lower case characters. An electronic full-ASCII keyboard should be used. Selectric keyboards are too inefficient—they can't keep up with a fast typist, there is no control character, and interface design is more complex than is the printer interface.

The manuscript for this book was processed on a system using a dual PerSci disk and Equinox-100 by Parasitic Engineering, an ADM3 terminal and a heavy-duty Selectric terminal. The software used was the standard CP/M editor. Some of the appendix was printed from a mailing list program.

In processing a manuscript you will have comments returning to you from the editor (and publisher), perhaps a co-author, as well as your own corrections and additions. These can be edited directly to your mass storage media, producing a final copy which is free of any markings or corrections. Self-published books can be updated with each printing.

Indexes can also be processed on your computer. Just enter the keywords and appropriate page numbers, letting your computer sort these alphabetically and identify the duplicates.

Software should always be listed from the stored copy for a camera-ready page. Do not retype, as there is too much chance for an error. If your printer is a dot matrix type, you can still use the output listing as it is in your book.

3 HOW TO OPERATE A SERVICE BUREAU

3.1 WHAT IS A SERVICE BUREAU?

A service bureau is a business established for selling computer time and closely allied support services. If the business sells processing time on a computer it is called a data processing service, though even secretarial services performed on word processing systems may be considered service bureau work, especially as the secretarial information-handling functions increase with more sophisticated systems.

The data processing service companies either sell you computer time for programs and data you bring to their shop, or you supply data to established programs run on their equipment. If you do a market analysis of these services in your city, you may find them using anything from an IBM 5100 to a time-shared Control Data system. They provide financial statements, sales analysis, address labels, modeling and simulation. Secretarial services provide a wide range of services, with the word processing system only a part of this support. Most will do typing (letters, manuscripts, resumes), address labels, mailing list processing, envelope stuffing, copying, small offset printing jobs and perhaps telephone answering.

Using the microcomputer, you can address a portion of the market covered by both of these businesses. You can also create new markets. Properly set up, you will discover that the depreciation and maintenance cost on your equipment is quite low, with your own labor being the primary cost factor.

3.2 CAN YOU COMPETE?

If you have a good computer system that is saving you money by doing your accounting and word processing, chances are you can use some of the system's free time to help others save money. You will have to ask yourself some hard questions and provide some realistic answers. You can start by analyzing the cost-effectiveness of your system. Does it really save you money if your labor and repair bills are included? The next thing to do is identify your saleable service. General-purpose services could include such things as a mailing list processing, letter processing, and accounting. You must either have or develop good support software in each of the areas you intend to market as a service.

As an example, you might consider offering an accounting* service. A simple accounting service might work well for your own business, but if you plan to offer it as a service, the software would need to include accounts receivable, accounts payable, general ledger, inventory, and payroll. In addition, the software must provide:

1. A good audit trail that will permit an auditor to trace any transactions.
2. A security level so that the files cannot be attained by unauthorized persons.
3. Full back-up files.
4. A good level of flexibility. For example, there are six ways to computer inventory, and you might want to use all six.

You also might want to include these features:

1. Do the bills or goods shipped match the goods ordered?
2. Can limits be established for fields?
3. Can check digits be used with account numbers?
4. How are controls provided to prevent cross-billing if the name is the same?
5. Are there checks for unwanted or unusual characters in some of the fields?

---

* You may choose to call this a "bookkeeping" service, no matter how complex and complete. Certain accounting functions can be offered only by registered, licensed accountants who can legally accept some responsibilities ordinary bookkeepers cannot.

To be able to offer this service you will also need reliable, fast, and efficient hardware. For instance, a 15-character-per-second Selectric might work for you, but for letters or mailing lists you will need at least 45 characters per second. You will need a video terminal with 24 lines of 80 characters each. Cassette storage or minidisks will not work. You will need a floppy disk storage and, if possible, also a hard disk. If possible, you should also use a 16-bit CPU, as the added speed will save you a good bit of time. You should be able to spool your output to the printer so you can continue working while the printer is outputting. Remember—your time will be the biggest cost factor to the customer. Maximize your productivity with careful hardware and software selection. Be sure the equipment is well made and reliable. Study the references in the Appendix for ideas on applications.

Once your hardware and software is defined, you will need to identify all of your costs and establish a fair price for your services. (See Table 3-1 for a description of these costs.) Some of these costs, such as supplies, can be well defined from your experience. Others, such as depreciation and repair, are more complex. A few trial runs will give you a good feel of how much labor is involved with various types of services. Be flexible at the start and keep accurate records. If you find that certain jobs take more time than others, charge more for them.

Hardware costs can best be calculated using the straight line depreciation method. This method can best be described with an example. Let's assume you have a system valued at $7,500. If you assume that your system has a seven-year lifetime and at the end of seven years you could sell it for $500, your depreciation is $1,000 per year. Now, let's assume that you use your computer about 15 hours a week. You cost per hour is about $1.28.

Repair costs primarily will involve mechanical repair. Typewriters are notorious for breaking down at just the wrong time. If possible, get a repair contract with either the manufacturer or a local office supply company.

Supplies can best be estimated by keeping track of what you actually use and adding 25 percent. When calculating these costs, do not forget to include separate floppy disks for your customers, and allow one back-up floppy for each one you expect to use. Keep the master disk for your software and the master customer data files in a safe deposit box at your bank or, if you can afford it, in a fireproof safe at home. One friend of ours had a recent burglary and discovered his unwanted visitor had sprayed the fire extinguisher on all his floppy disks. The damage was not covered by his insurance. The cost of the safe deposit box, your desk, filing cabinets, and other office supplies should be included in your price. Total your costs for a typical service plus your profit. For convenience, you might want to use a formula for figuring out prices. You may identify these costs in a mailing list job:

Item	Cost
Computer time 4 hrs. @ $1.28	$ 5.12
Software $10.00	10.00
Development time $10.00	10.00
Floppy disks 2 @ $6.00	12.00
Supplies $4.00	4.00
Office furniture, etc. $3.00	3.00
Profit	10.00
	$54.12

You would be much better off using a simple "4 times" formula. Simply add the computer time and the development time together and multiply by 4, giving you a price of $60.48. Another idea would be to charge your customers a flat rate for each item. For instance, you could charge 20¢ for entering a name into the file and 10¢ for each label produced. If the above project produced 200 labels the first time and 200 each time thereafter, your charges would be $60 for the first run and $20 for each run thereafter. Both you and your customer would be happier with this method. Be sure you do not get so many variables in your routine cost calculations that your calculations become overly complex. You might also compare your prices with the local service bureau. Can you provide the same service in the same or better time, and can you offer these services at the same or better price? If so, you can compete.

3.3 SOME ACTUAL CASE HISTORIES AND SOME IDEAS

Turnaround time is an important factor in your service. In some cases your customer may be willing to pay extra for fast service. For instance, we know a real estate broker who was presented with a tremendous opportunity that depended upon the accessibility of information. He was able to acquire a list of

TABLE 3-1 SERVICE BUREAU COSTS

Computer system depreciation

Program and software costs (application software, BASIC, and CP/M costs?)

Service and maintenance

Supplies (paper, carbons, labels, envelopes, floppies)

Labor (Payroll)

    Set-up charges (master letter form or inputting a mailing list)

    Computer operation charges (processing against previously established files)

    File update charges (altering mailing lists or data, proofing letters)

Overhead

    Taxes (local, state, federal)

    Business license fee

    Utilities (rental, utilities, garbage)

    Rent and upkeep

    Safe deposit box

    Insurance

    Gas, automobile and travel

Professional organizations, magazines, conferences

---

a hundred property owners whose property would change status due to a new zoning ordinance. Some of these property owners would want to sell right away. The broker needed to act quickly before other brokers contacted these people. He wanted to send individually addressed and signed letters to all his prospects immediately. We were able to do the entire list in one day, making his customers happy and gaining a new client. The key selling point here was the time saved with the computer. You can make the most of opportunities like this after you establish a reputation for fair prices and prompt service. You'll have to work at establishing a reputation and also let people know that you exist. Using the method described in Section 3.2, establish a price schedule. Design a brochure that describes your services and have it printed. Make use of this brochure and other sales techniques which are covered fully in Chapter 10. Pay careful attention to marketing your service as well.

    Price is an important consideration in selling your services, so you should analyze your prices carefully. In some cases you can quote on a per-hour basis. A letter, for example, might include a $2.50 set-up charge per page for the first letter and 60¢ per page for additional letters with only the address altered. Mailing lists could be quoted on a per-hundred basis, with set-up charged separately.

You will need some practice before you will be able to firmly establish your prices. As a start, you might offer to process your computer club's newsletter or help a church with some mailing. This will give you a good check on your calculations. Are your prices realistic for the labor involved?

Once you establish a set of basic services, you can then broaden your scope to include additional services. Local golf clubs or bowling leagues might be willing to invest some of their club money into score calculations. You might even want to set up your system in a van and drive to various tournaments, offering statistical service on a real-time basis.

The largest market for services is neglected customers— someone else's. Service bureaus' tendency to overlook small customers should provide you with a golden opportunity. Some people who have never considered using a computer in their business might consider it, if you approach them in the right manner. Look for service applications not being met by large service bureaus. As an example, we know a bookstore supplier who had trouble getting paid by some of the bookstores he supplied. The smaller stores sometimes went bankrupt paying off only the larger publishers and wholesalers. He was always far down the list and seldom got anything. Using some of our computer time, he proposed to network the small suppliers together and identify accounts that were past due over 30 or 60 days. Using the computer, he could keep this list always up to date and sell it on a subscription basis. The microcomputer was ideal for this, and the program development was quite simple.

Chances are that your service bureau customers will soon become good clients for a systems sale and a maintenance contract. Your service bureau then becomes part of your total support package. If his system crashes, you can not only repair the system but can offer him temporary service bureau support while he is waiting.

3.4 A PROJECT YOU CAN START ON IMMEDIATELY

Other than inadequate cash or improper cash management, the major cause of failure for small bookstores is improper inventory management. This is a problem that can be readily solved by a computer. Generally, bookstore managers have no idea of what sells and what does not. A typical store might carry 200 titles. Of these, they will probably have five or six copies of each title and ten or more of a select few. Yet, an analysis of their sales records will show that they will seldom sell more than three or four copies per month of any title and an average of one copy a month of most titles. Good business sense would indicate that if the manager has an inventory of 1,000 books, he should tie it up in 800 or more titles rather than 200.

You can help him by setting up an inventory analysis program. All books now have a special identifying number called an ISBN (International Standard Book Number). This number is assigned to the publisher for each individual book, so each number is unique. You can identify the store inventory by both title and ISBN. Each book in the store could have a card inserted with the ISBN on it. When the book is sold, the card can be put in a separate box. Once or twice a week these cards can be sent to you. At the end of the month you can produce an inventory that shows what has been sold. You can even generate the required purchase orders.

This is just one of many opportunities available to you if you keep an open mind. Once you have developed an inventory management program for a small bookstore, you might try a hardware store, or a clothing store, or? Opportunity is where you find it!

3.5 FINDING A LOCATION

Locate near your market. One local copyist we know has made good money by opening a series of small copying stores around the business area of town. Businessmen can walk to his store and get their copies while they wait. Your turnaround time may be longer, but the strategy is the .same. Take your business to the market. A home-based service bureau can create problems with the local zoning codes if you get much traffic. You will have to pick up and deliver most of your work. The third alternative would be a small van with the computer inside, taking your store to the "market"—in this case, a golf or bowling tournament.

3.6 EXPOSURE AND SECURITY

You will often be processing sensitive and confidential material. In some cases, you might even be asked to provide service for a project that is illegal or unethical. You will need to establish a policy on customer relations and ethics. What happens if you lose confidential data? Will you refuse certain types of jobs?

It would be wise to work with a lawyer to prepare a standard contract for your customers. You also should have a clean business area with a good filing system that can be locked and which permits rapid access to your customers' files. The level of security also will be determined by your customer base. What market are you trying to attract?

Be sure all files are duplicated periodically and placed in a safe deposit box.

3.7 SO YOU HAVE NO FREE TIME?

Maybe you have no free time, but your computer still sits idle several hours each day. Why not sell this computer time to others? Your costs can be quite low, as your only expenses will be computer depreciation and maintenance. The user brings his own supplies and maintains responsibility for the integrity of his data.

We have met several people who cannot afford an expensive system but can spend about $100 a month developing software products they wish to sell. Once their product is returning some income, they will have money to purchase their system. You can help them bootstrap themselves into the wonderful world of computers. The user should prepay for a block of time. You can give him a short course on how to use the system, after which he is on his own.

3.8 SMORGASBOARD

A computer professional once told us that his kids have a thriving business going with their home computer selling Star Trek computer time to the local neighborhood kids. Children are extremely creative and if you turn yours loose with the home system, they might even pay their own way through college. Their minds are less bent by our behavioral conditioning.

Look for unusual contests and do not hesitate to apply your computer. Remember those college kids in California that used a computer to win the McDonald's contest? At one computer faire we attended, one of the booths offered numbered tickets to those attending their booth, offering a prize if you could find someone with a matching number. Some enterprising kids were picking up tickets from the floor and using some computer time in one of the booths to track these tickets and find matches. They ended up with several prizes.

If you like contests from your home, write (sending a self-addressed and stamped envelope) to Micropuzzle, 7858 Canteloupe Avenue, Van Nuys, CA 91402. With most contests, there is no need to tell the friendly folks that you plan to use your computer to win. You can also create puzzles with the computer and sell these to magazines and newspapers.

Use your imagination with your personal skills and interests to study Table 3-2. What application areas interest you? Can you build hardware products, software products, or services around this application area? New applications for the microcomputer will emerge in your own community daily. Why not start one yourself?

Bartering Service–Use your computer to match needs and resources at a community level.

Real Estate–Use the computer to give brokers real-time listings of property for sale.

Equipment Rental Service–Help your community to pool their equipment resources, using the computer to match people who have equipment to rent with those who have a need for such equipment.

Shoppers' Guide (to apartment, medical, or automotive repair)–Use the computer to give real-time access to customers on product (or service) availability and quality.

Clothing Clearinghouse–The computer monitors clothing outgrown by the user but with good wear left.

Babysitting Referral Service–The computer lists sitters available on short notice.

Calling Service–Receive calls, make calls, or monitor messages.

Office Services–Mailing lists, proposals, and letters done quickly.

Classified Newsletter–Low-cost newsletter of community items available for sale (real-time garage sale!).

TABLE 3-2 MICROCOMPUTER APPLICATION AREAS

budget analysis	routine correspondence
general ledger	proposals and manuscripts
invoicing	filling out forms
payroll	statistical analysis
accounts receivable	correlation studies
accounts payable	polls, surveys
sorting	packing lists
mailing lists and addressing	inventory
shopping lists	sales analysis
meal analysis	travel planning
meal planning	editing
taxes	filing
education	information retrieval
community memory	needs/resource matching
electronic bartering	handicaps and game scoring
electronic message handling	simulations (energy,
games	political, etc.)
electronic design	music synthesis
stock market analysis	selling tickets
tickler files (reminder notes)	nursing home systems
project planning	resource management
card catalogs (library,	sensor/control systems
cassette, records, etc.)	garden planning

Apartment or House Rentals—Monitor available housing, location and costs.

Computer Leasing—Rent your equipment for short-term projects.

Computer Center—Open a store with a dozen systems, both cassette and disk based. Sell time on systems, family memberships, and classes.

Now it's your turn! As a creative exercise, try to add as many items as you can to this list and Table 3-2. Mark the ideas that excite you the most and begin your journey!

4 HOW TO OPERATE A COMPUTER REPAIR BUSINESS

With the sale of home computers increasing rapidly, it is easy to understand the growing need for specialists who can repair the large variety of systems being sold. This rush of small systems sales promises to bring great benefits to very small businesses.

All this activity, however, has raised some serious questions: Where will we find the people to install, maintain, and repair these systems?

The number of people in the field today, coupled with the number entering each year, will not provide nearly enough technicians to fill the need over the next ten years. One alternative, self-diagnosing computers, is too far off in the future to help. Even the so-called "turnkey" systems require considerable systems effort to serve a company's needs. Add to this the fact that many computers will be sold through retail department stores where the salesman knows little or nothing about the product, and you have a real problem. As a general rule, retail stores cannot afford the time required for repairs or the space to stock repair parts. In addition, repair people, though "expert" in such things as televisions, washing machines, or hi-fi systems, will have little or no training in computers. Even the manufacturers will not be economically able to support the consumer. Why should a manufacturer send a part to a customer who buys only one, when they could put the same part in a $1,000 machine?

This means there is a growing opportunity for technicians who have the proper background and a little capital. Can you qualify? First, you will need a solid grounding in computer electronics. If you need some additional work in this area, there are many books you could study. For instance, you might want to look at *Analysis and Design of Digital Circuits and Computer Systems*, by Chirlian, published by Matrix. You also will need a background in working with small systems. You can gain some of this experience by working with a retail computer store. They will be delighted to have you offer your service at a modest rate, and you can spend your time assembling and testing as many systems as possible. Read everything you can get your hands on. For instance, *Byte* magazine comes as close to a technical journal for small systems as you will find anywhere. Another book that will help you is, *Introduction to Microprocessor Systems Engineering*, by Camp, Smay and Triska, published by Matrix.

4.1 WHAT YOU WILL NEED TO GET STARTED

To start your business, you will need a good stock of test instruments, typical electronic cards, and diagnostic software (Table 5-1). The spare cards should use switches instead of jumpers. This allows you to select the starting memory address on the memory cards of the port on the I/O cards; otherwise you will be resoldering your jumpers on every repair call. The oscilloscope should be a high-quality scope with dual traces and sufficient speed to see TTL logic. For software, use simple diagnostic routines that are loaded from tapes, using your own cassette tape card and a PROM card. You should also try to obtain both a PET and a TRS-80 computer, as the volume of both of these products will merit some repair support.

Don't waste your time trying to repair systems on site. You can adopt a modular repair concept by using your program to identify the ailing card. If possible, replace the problem card with one of yours and take it back to the shop, giving your customer little or no down time. You might even want to use a van as a mobile repair shop. Once you repair the customer's card, it can be replaced in his system. Be sure to maintain a professional image so your customer will have confidence in your abilities. If you need to scratch your head about the problem, it is best to do it in your own shop rather than in front of your customer.

If the problem is mechanical, you may have to contract it out to someone experienced with the mechanism. If you cannot repair something confidently, you should be able to refer it to someone who can. Typewriters and printers usually fall into this category. You should maintain a list of skilled repair people who you know you can count on. Deal with them yourself and pay them separately. They will appreciate it, and you will be able to provide a total service to your customers.

Diagnostic software is very important. You should design flexible and simple software that enables you to quickly locate the defective board in a variety of environments. These programs can be loaded from cassette tape and be carried in a tape caddy of the type used for audio cassettes. They should be clearly labeled and you should keep at least one set of back-up tapes in a safe, separate location.

Floppies are a different problem. Most require a special test instrument to align and repair. This instrument is expensive and will work for only one manufacturer's product. The best approach is to air freight a defective drive directly to the manufacturer. The dual-density disks and the large variety of controllers make this problem increasingly difficult to control. Unfortunately, the only sane approach for you is to provide a back-up system. This is expensive, but it gives you the opportunity to provide a service few others will undertake.

Many times the repair will be a simple oversight. He may have forgotten to plug in the system (yes, that happens!), or he may have blown a fuse, or he may have misread how to use the software. Sometimes you can handle these problems by telephone. It will also give you a great opportunity to sell your customer on the idea of a long-term service contract.

4.2 WHAT TO CHARGE

Service can be sold from a variety of approaches. Some customers may want to pay you for each call. Typical prices today vary from $20 to $35 per hour plus parts. Other customers may want to purchase a service contract from you. Basically, this means that you agree to perform all servicing on the equipment for a flat monthly fee. Contracts should sell for about 1 percent of the system cost per month, or about $100 to $500 a month, depending on the size of the system. Since most systems are quite reliable, the customer will generally save money by paying on a per-call basis. Other variables you will need to consider are:

1. Whether you will pick up and deliver systems, and how this will affect your service costs.
2. Whether you will provide 24-hour service, and the cost for this.
3. Whether you will provide loaners, and the cost (if any) of these.

For more details on how stores are pricing their repair services, see Portia Isaacson's column in the August 1978 issue of *Datamation.*

Initially, you should not commit yourself to service contracts of more than three months so that you will have an opportunity to clearly evaluate your costs. Be sure to have an attorney read through your service contract and advise you as to your obligations. (See Appendix C for a sample service agreement.)

Try to provide as much service as possible. Develop a strategy for quickly getting to your customer. Use an answering service and pick up your messages frequently. Keep careful records of all your repair work indexed by customers and systems. This will help you see the relationship between cause and effect. Soon you will be able to do preventive maintenance and reduce your servicing costs. This is especially important for those customers who have a service contract. Remember to do first-rate work, even if it costs you money. A service business is only as good as the service it provides.

4.3 USING THE COMPUTER

The computer can manage information flow in your store. Use it to monitor systems and repair equipment for preventive maintenance. The computer also can monitor your inventory, process your payroll, update the general ledger, and generate your statements.

Customers can be monitored through a mailing list program. Embedded codes can identify every component of each customer's system, and the mailing list can be used to mail brochures. If you have a used I/O board that only fits a particular system, you can profile an advertisement to only those customers who have that equipment.

4.4 WILL THE REPAIR STORE SURVIVE?

There is a growing concern on the part of computer retailers to service what they sell. Reliability on the better systems is so good that stores can offer repair contracts for practically nothing or offer a discount on repairs for equipment they sell to force the independent repairman out of the market.

The independent repairman, however, is here to stay. Many stores may offer repair, but it may not be quality repair at a professional level. Independent repairmen can also improve their chance of survival by increasing their repair base. A few ideas for this expansion may include:

1. Repairing audio equipment, television, or citizen's band equipment from an electronic repair supermarket.
2. Doing engineering and development such as altering peripherals for microcomputer systems.
3. Repairing systems and peripherals not well supported locally.
4. Repairing one or more of the popular minicomputer systems.
5. Offering features which local stores will not provide, such as free loaners, repair on premises, or fast turnaround time.

You may also find local retail stores that want to get out of servicing in order to provide more space for demonstrators and equipment. The store makes money on equipment sales, not repair contracts. By contracting with the store to service what they sell, you permit them to do more of what they do best—selling systems.

Remember, manufacturers always want strong service support in areas where their machines are sold. Turnaround time is important. If repair support for a good system is weak in your area, this means a good opportunity for you to work directly with the manufacturer in providing service.

5 HOW TO DEVELOP AND SELL YOUR SOFTWARE

There is one indisputable fact about the software business: The market is wide open, with the saturation point nowhere in sight during the next few years. There are virtually unlimited possibilities in the hobby, personal, business, and scientific markets. Software is the fastest growing segment of the data processing industry, and you can cash in on it.

5.1 THE CHANGING SOFTWARE MARKET

In the early decades of the computer industry, basic software ordinarily was provided by the hardware manufacturer in a package with the equipment. The institutions buying the equipment did their own applications software or hired experts to write custom programs for them. As the numbers of computers increased, government restrictions and market demand forced the hardware companies to price software as a separate entity, thus creating a new and fast-growing market.

About 1975 a new kind of software market based on microcomputer system began to emerge. This was due, in part, to the difference in architecture of this software. Theory manuals for software design had to be rewritten, and programmers had to learn many new techniques. For instance, a sort algorithm on an IBM system might be designed for speed, a large core, and virtual storage on a fast, hard disk. The microcomputer system might involve only 32,000 bytes of storage and a slow floppy disk handling just a small mailing list. Word processing software written in BASIC that justifies quickly on a DEC minicomputer system might run entirely too slowly on a microcomputer system. These problems have created a need for not only new software development techniques but new software marketing techniques.

The marketing concepts for software developed before 1975 are not adequate for the age of microcomputers. Minicomputers and large-system software have traditionally been sold through elaborate licensing agreements. Sales volumes are low and the prices are high. The marketing strategy for microcomputers is low price and high volume. For instance, a high-quality CP/M operating system is considered the industry standard. It usually sells for only $100, including documentation.

A large variety of companies is publishing software in books, on tape cassettes, and on floppy disks. A partial list of these companies appears in Appendix H. Use the same care in selecting a software publisher as you would in selecting a book publisher. Find out as much as you can about royalty agreements and the company's ability to market the software. Remember: if the company cannot market your software aggressively, the royalty rate is insignificant.

5.2 SOFTWARE LEGAL ISSUES

Legal protection for software is a real problem. Software cannot be patented; it is a simple matter to get around the copyright. The function can be reproduced if the program is slightly altered. Only direct, line-for-line source codes cannot be copied. Several approaches have been used for additional protection:

1. Keep the cost so low that the cost of copying the software is not justified.
2. Use license agreements. (See Appendix D.)
3. Avoid selling the source listing.
4. Include a serial number with all software in the disk or cassette software files. This makes it possible to trace any black market copy to the initial customer.

Some software maufacturers use all four approaches, but with limited success. A new approach to protecting software has recently evolved: publish the software in book form; it is then protected by the book's copyright.

Another legal problem you might encounter is protecting yourself against liabilities from the use of your software. If you sell accounting software to a company that has inadequate protection against user mistakes, they might sue you for their losses. Do you provide adequate audit trails and entry checks? Even worse, imagine what would happen if the company discovered an error in the software file management. Over the next few years, you can expect software users to become more demanding in what they expect from suppliers. You can partially avoid this pitfall by having a firm agreement with the customer that states your exact liabilities. In addition, careful management and documentation of your software will prevent most problems. (See Appendix D for a sample software sales agreement.)

5.3 SOFTWARE EVALUATION

Software evaluation is a problem area that can provide you with an opportunity. Most of the microcomputer BASICs have been reviewed and compared in the major magazines. However, application software, particularly for business, is sold on a "buyer beware" basis. This would be a good opportunity for a magazine article, but the cost of purchasing the software would be many times the return.

You can provide a much-needed service by providing these software evaluations. A user planning to spend $2,000 for a good software accounting package would be quite willing to spend $100 for an evaluation of all accounting systems in the microcomputer market. You even may be able to obtain a copy of each manufacturer's software, at no charge, for evaluation purposes.

5.4 DEFINE YOUR MARKET

There are many different software markets. Before you start developing software, identify the general market you hope to reach. The hobby market and various professional markets have entirely different needs. For instance, a bookkeeper may have a hard time trying to use a hobbyist program. The bookkeeper wants something that guides him through the procedures, while a hobbyist may be interested in space utilization and cost. Some of the differences in these markets are outlined in Table 5-1.

Some markets are showing signs of saturation (such as Star Trek), but most offer wide opportunities. Do not be discouraged if someone develops a program similar to yours. Software

**TABLE 5-1 The Hobby Market Versus the Professional
Software Market**

Hobby Software Market	Professional Software Market
Low cost	More concern with cost effectiveness (will it save us money?)
Commentaries and prompts can be minimal. More concern with minimal memory use	Very user oriented. Must be easy to use by someone unfamiliar with software. Programs can be longer with plenty of prompt comments.
Enough documentation to run the program, but not enough to increase the price too much	Must be well documented with maintenance and update support. Documentation must be professionally done.

development is something like writing books on elementary programming: there seems to be an unending market for it. Some software needs are shown in Tables 5-2, 5-3 and 5-4; two of these possibilities are expanded and amplified in Tables 5-5 and 5-6.

TABLE 5-2: HOBBYIST SOFTWARE POSSIBILITIES

1. Video enhancements to current games
2. High-level language for game development
3. Community networking programs (people/people)
4. Information retrieval programs (people/information)
5. New games
6. Computer versions of older games
7. Simulations and modeling (energy, economics, resources)
8. Using the computer for polling on issues and voting
9. Nutrition analysis
10. Electronic mail and message switching
11. Biorhythms
12. Checkbook and home bookkeeping
13. Bowling scores
14. Home energy usage
15. Educational programs

TABLE 5-3: BUSINESS SOFTWARE POSSIBILITIES

1. Stock market analyzers
2. Full business accounting packages (G/L, A/R, A/P, inventory, payroll)
3. Real estate multilistings
4. Word processors (with justifying and automatic spelling correction!)
5. Mailing list processors (with letter processors)
6. Medical history programs
7. Medical billing programs
8. Inventory control
9. Investment analysis (real estate)
10. Management control programs (time schedules, costs, project flow, etc.)
11. Nursing home management and control programs
12. Market research
13. Automatic telephone dialing
14. Sales analysis
15. Salesman's tickler file

TABLE 5-4: UTILITY SOFTWARE POSSIBILITIES

1. Diagnostic software (disk, memory, I/O and CPU testing)
2. Data base management and file management software
3. Sorting software
4. High-level languages
5. Preprocessors for existing languages
6. I/O modules for existing products, such as I/O spoolers, modem drivers, etc.
7. Converters and simulators (converting one CPU language to another)

5.5 DEFINE YOUR PRODUCT

Writing software can be quite similar to writing an article. The first step in writing a good article is to develop an outline; the software equivalent of an outline is the specification sheet. Laid out properly, it shows the peripherals required, the memory

TABLE 5-5: MAILING LIST PROGRAM FEATURES

1. Sorts on any field permitting, with file merges permitted before sorts.
2. Embedded multi-character codes for extraction purposes. Extracted files can be created.
3. Boolean operations permitted on extraction codes, zips, and titles for extracted files.
4. Updating feature permits finding addresses by searching on any field. Character and line editing on updating.
5. Added addresses can be prefixed or suffixed in file without resorting.
6. Printing can be started or stopped at any point in the file.
7. Directory listing of file can be printed, as well as file scans without printing.
8. Envelopes and multi-column labels may be printed. Full form control on label printing.
9. Form letter module:
   a. embedded stops in letter
   b. automatic greeting
   c. embedded format control in text permitted
   d. automatic justification if desired
   e. envelope printing with letter

required, module run time, cost, special features, and module description.

Table 5-7 shows a specification sheet for a mailing list program. The specification sheet should be developed carefully and referred to often. It can be used as a marketing tool once you have completed your product.

Professional software is usually marketed and, more often than not, sold as part of a system. In the near future, most microcomputer software will be sold in book form, providing documentation and source listings. Canned programs on cassettes and floppy disks will be prepared to accompany these books. In fact, there is already a burgeoning market for cassette software.

Unlike the minicomputer and large-system software, there will be little continuing relationship between the user and supplier. For instance, if you sell software for a large system, you have a contract that spells out your rights and obligations. Your rights and obligations can include the level of performance

TABLE 5-6: WORD PROCESSING PROGRAM FEATURES

1. Automatic left and right margin changes
2. Automatic justification to any specified line length
3. Control on paragraph assembly
4. Automatic centering
5. Automatic hyphenation at end of lines
6. Automatic underscoring
7. Automatic table of contents
8. Global, line, and character editing
9. Automatic paging and page headings
10. Multi-column, with each column justified
11. Stored glossary
12. Merge and block move features
13. Automatic formatting
14. Automatic decimal alignment
15. Move and copy features
16. Extensive formatting control on printing

expected, level of documentation, update and maintenance responsibilities, license agreements, third-party restrictions, payment specifications, damage and liability responsibilities, and delivery time. (Whew!)

Supplying software for microcomputer systems is far simpler. However, if you plan direct sales without publishing your software in book form, you will need to use your specification sheet as your "contract." A sample direct mail piece that can be used for this purpose is shown in Table 5-8.

5.6 DEFINE YOUR LANGUAGE

Selecting a language in which to write your program is almost as important as deciding what you are going to produce. You can write the greatest program in the world, but if it isn't in a form usable by a wide variety of people, it is essentially valueless. Assembly language programs are the most effective in terms of computer memory and speed. However, development expense is high and, due to the inflexibility of the program, modifications and updates are difficult.

The most widely used microcomputer language is BASIC. The language has several advantages for you and your customers.

TABLE 5-7: MAILOUT SPECIFICATION SHEET

Hardware Required: Microprocessor (8080, 6800, Z80, etc.)
                     48K or more of memory
                     video terminal (serial interface)
                     printer (pin or tractor feed)
                     floppy disk mass storage

Software Required: CP/M operating system version 1.3 or 1.4
                     Microsoft BASIC or Commercial BASIC
                     (CBASIC) (specify BASIC in ordering)

MODULES SUPPLIED:

BUILD —   Constructs mailing list files. Addresses can contain any number of embedded single-character codes that do not print on labels but permit creation of subfiles (as active or inactive membership, magazine expiration date, or subject coding).

SORT —   Sorts on address/title or zip code. Can also be used to merge files.

LIST —   Prints labels or envelopes. Labels can be printed in single or multiple columns. LIST can start or end at special zips or addresses, or extract on mailing list codes for printing only a portion of a file.

CLIST —   Prints full file directory with embedded mailing list codes for file purposes.

UPDATE —   Updates mailing list files. Locates addresses by address/title and permits changes. Addresses can also be added to the file with UPDATE, using suffix and prefix modes bypassing time-consuming sorts.

EXTRACT —   Permits creation of subfiles by extraction on zip codes, mailing list codes, address/title range, or zip code range.

LETTER —   Processes multiple letters against an address file.

HELP —   Prints general directions.

TABLE 5-8: THE BROCHURE

Center for the Study of the Future
4110 N. E. Alameda
Portland, OR 97212
503-282-5835

Hardware Required: Microprocessor (8080, 6800, Z80, etc)
48K or more of memory
video terminal (serial interface)
printer (pin or tractor feed)
floppy disk mass storage

Software Required: CP/M operating system version 1.3 or 1.4
Microsoft BASIC or Commercial BASIC
(CBASIC) (specify BASIC in ordering)

MODULES SUPPLIED:

BUILD —   Constructs mailing list files. Addresses can contain any number of embedded single-character codes that do not print on labels but permit creation of subfiles (as active or inactive membership, magazine expiration date, or subject coding).

SORT —   Sorts on address/title or zip code. Can also be used to merge files.

LIST —   Prints labels or envelopes. Labels can be printed in single or multiple columns. LIST can start or end at special zips or addresses, or extract on mailing list codes for printing only a portion of the file.

CLIST —   Prints full file directory with embedded mailing list codes for file purposes.

UPDATE —   Updates mailing list files. Locates addresses by address/title and permits changes. Addresses can also be added to the file with UPDATE, using suffix and prefix modes bypassing time-consuming sorts.

EXTRACT — Permits creation of subfiles by extraction on zip codes, mailing list codes, address/title range, or zip code range.

LETTER —   Processes multiple letters against an address file.
HELP —   Prints general directions.

Cost:	$75 on 8″ floppy disk with documentation and source code
	$5 User's Manual only (no source code)
	Specify source code desired (Microsoft BASIC or Commercial BASIC). Orders shipped COD or prepaid only.
Delivery:	Immediate

First, it is a relatively easy language to learn, so a lot of your customers will be familiar with it. Due to the flexibility of the language, software development costs and product development time both are low.

BASIC is an excellent overall language that can be used for most of your applications; however, there are some problems. One problem is that there is no standard BASIC. A program written for one BASIC may not run in a different system without considerable modification. BASIC is also quite slow in doing sorts and string searches. It is also difficult to use structured programming techniques. Even with its problems, BASIC is probably the best language for small programs.

Other high-level langauges, such as FORTRAN, APL, PASCAL, and COBOL, offer the best opportunities for future programming developments. For instance, although FORTRAN is weak in string processing, it is possible to build library routines to process strings. These subroutines then can be called for a variety of application programs such as word processing, mailing list processing, and keyword information retrieval. The final compiler output is in assembly level coding, runs very fast, and can be sold without the source. At least one data management system for microcomputer systems is already available in FORTRAN. It has a large number of support subroutines for split-screen display and string processing and sells for $2,000.

A programmer should be able to write about nine lines of code per hour on short programs and three lines of code per hour on longer, more complex programs. This rate is independent of the type of language used. A line of FORTRAN, however, expands to many lines of assembly-level coding. High-level programs are, therefore, most cost effective to develop. Assembly-level programs run faster and use less memory. Even though they will take you longer to develop, an assembly-level program will be a better product and offer you a more competitive advantage.

Preprocessors exist for some of the languages, as in FORTRAN, thus expanding their usage. A word processor can be written in a highly structured language of a preprocessor, converted to FORTRAN, and then to assembly level coding. Only the final object code is sold with an embedded serial number. If the user needs modifications, these are requested when the order is placed for the program or can be purchased later. For information on using a preprocessor, see *Software Tools*, by Kernigham and Plauger, Addison Wesley Publishing Company, 1976.

5.7 DEVELOPING YOUR PROGRAM

If you develop your program using structured programming techniques, you'll save yourself a lot of headaches. The primary advantage of structured programming is the modular approach, which makes documentation and maintenance much easier. In addition, you can borrow these modules for subsequent program development.

It is also a good idea to use data-base management concepts whenever and wherever possible. This will give you a method of creating common files among all of your programs. For instance, you might be able to use a mailing list file for a word processor program. This has the advantages of cutting down on your development time and improving your sales base.

Once you are satisfied with your program, you will be ready to prepare a user's manual. Be sure your user's manual is non-technical; assume the user knows very little about computers or programming. Be sure to show things like printouts, video dialogue and anything else that may be helpful. Regardless of how you plan to publish the user's manual, read Chapter 2 before you prepare it.

6 HOW TO DEVELOP AND SELL YOUR HARDWARE

If you have some experience in electronics and a creative idea for a new computer product, there is plenty of opportunity in developing and marketing hardware. Most of the major microcomputer companies started in garages just a few years ago. Although this is not as easy today, there is still a considerable market for peripheral devices of all types.

As a rule, you will find that technology leads application: someone invents the product and applications emerge as people begin to use it. But what are the chances that your product will succeed? Remember this: no one really envisioned the possibilities of the microcomputer when it was introduced. Major companies, such as Radio Shack, Heath, Digital Equipment Corporation and IBM, could have been, but were not first with microcomputers. They simply didn't see an advantage in being first, so it's doubtful that they will see the advantage of being first with various peripherals.

6.1 IDEAS FOR PRODUCTS

Here are just a few possibilities for new product areas:

1. Produce a current product on the market at a lower cost. Often this can be done by using a higher level of integration in the electronics. (The first company to introduce a one-chip video terminal at a very low cost will capture a large market. Why can't the daisy wheel printer with only eight moving parts be made for $600?)

2. Improve an existing product. (How about a video terminal with a good keyboard instead of the wiper contacts? How about a good low-cost, high quality printer?)
3. Create a new product.

One of the strongest product development areas for the near future is hardware that enhances communication between the user and the system. The computer needs to be "humanized" with more tangible, satisfying feedback as the machine is used. As an example, we recently improved our system functionally by going to a better buss, a larger power supply, and actively terminating our buss lines. The system is controlled from a special keyboard with EPROM software and LED display. Performance is much better, but there is one problem: we miss the flashing lights on the ol' Altair! The movement and flashing of lights gave life to the system.

Current products in this area include such things as joy sticks, light pens, turtles, and speech synthesizers. Chips are already available that can create a variety of game sounds, but you can create circuits that do more. How about an input device that makes sound, can be squeezed, has a definite texture, or lights up? Some product possibilities are shown in Table 6-1.

TABLE 6-1: HARDWARE PRODUCT POSSIBILITIES

1. Communication enhancements between the user and the computer
2. Sensor and controls for home use (fire alarms, burglar alarms, energy control, emergency automatic telephone dialing)
3. Small special-purpose business systems with software for applciation areas as nursing homes, pharmacists, medical history, lumber mills, etc.
4. Unusual games and simulations
5. Robots (special-purpose units are feasible now!)
6. Electronic message centers (telephone interface and cable television interfaces)
7. Music synthesizers, special hardware for music and hi-fi systems, or sound generators

6.2 FUNDING ALTERNATIVES

Developing a hardware product takes money—and lots of it. If you have the money, you have a distinct advantage. If you do not have capital, there are three alternatives in launching your product:

1. Obtain venture capital, offering in return a portion of your stock.
2. Bootstrap your operation from near-zero capital to the final market.
3. Sell your idea to a manufacturer.

Several manufacturers are currently using a fourth approach that borders on fraud, and is loaded with risk: they advertise the product, collect money from customers, and use this cash as capital for developing the product and the business. A bad practice! Customers are getting smarter—particularly the businessmen who are now the primary system buyers. We highly advise *not* advertising products until you have a firm delivery date.

The second option may work successfully in getting your product ready for the market, but a successful marketing program may easily require $30,000. Initial product sales will not be fast enough to obtain this capital and stay ahead of your competitors. If you can borrow some test equipment and have enough money to purchase the components you need for development, you will probably find it worthwhile to bootstrap yourself through your development. Once you have your product developed, you can go after venture capital. In this way you will have a working example of your product and can put yourself in a favorable position with investors.

The third option is a viable alternative if you are very creative and need to move on to other ideas and products. Going for venture capital is risky, time consuming, and may not be as exciting to you as moving on to the next idea. If this is you, sell the idea and start creating again. Decide whether you are a technologist or a business executive—or both.

The first approach is the suggested alternative for most people, as venture capital for microcomputer applications has been relatively easy to obtain.

Many entrepreneurs today are beginning to choose this first approach in obtaining their capital, and it is a sound business practice. You will gain, however, by developing the product as much as possible before you try to sell someone on helping you.

6.3 GETTING VENTURE CAPITAL

Before you attempt to get money from businessmen who know little about you, be sure you have exhausted your own resources. The first question most venture capitalists will ask is, "How much are you risking?" If you aren't risking your own resources, how can you expect someone else to risk his?

The moral is simple: Tap all available resources before attempting to sell your idea to venture capitalists. Can you refinance your house? Can you get money from relatives? How about friends? After you have exhausted all these resources and find you still need money, then, and only then, can you turn to venture capitalists, either institutions or individuals.

The venture capitalist is interested in only one thing: a good return on his investment. A return of five times the investment in three years or ten times the investment in five years is expected. The Qume printer, for example, returned thirty times the investment in five years.

Ordinarily, the investor doesn't want to bother with the responsibility of management. He wants to put his money to work under a good manager (you?) who shares his risk. Individuals may be genuinely interested in your product or ideas and can bring management skills in along with the money. Institutional investors, however, responsible for the profitable management of millions of dollars, can't spend the time.

This means you must come up with a plan which has profit as its goal, and the plan should show how you expect to reach your goal. Typically, the time line of the plan should show four periods:

1. Complete development of the product
2. Reaching the break-even point
3. Producing at a profit
4. Concluding the plan (selling the stock and letting the venture capitalist out with a profit)

Indeed, a good business plan/projection will plot your expected expenditures and income month by month for two years, then quarter by quarter for another couple years, showing break-even operation inside two years. Of course, it is nonsense to believe that this speculation will match reality, but the investor wants to know that you are actually planning realistically and he wants some standard by which you and he can measure your performance.

An idea man often is not a good manger. In other words, as much as you would like to get into the company and *manage* the product, it is generally a bad idea. Unless you have a track record, you will have a hard time selling yourself as a manager of funds. Most institutional venture capitalists do not invest in anything under $300,000. They like big ideas and high-quality people to pull off the idea. Few venture capitalists are really venturesome—what they really want is a sure thing, dressed up in risky language. Do you look like a sure thing? If you wish to be involved, place yourself on the board; be a secretary or treasurer and learn as much as you can. Keep your salary low. Your profit should come at the end when the goal is reached, not from living off the money of others. You are risking, along with your venture capitalists. They will get most of the profit, but you should still see a large profit on what you invest.

6.4 THE BUSINESS PLAN

Regardless of the strategy, you need a solid business plan. An outline you can use as a guideline for drawing up the plan is shown in Table 6-2. Take the time to think through and organize this plan, even if you do not plan to go after venture capitalists.

Note well that there are a million ways to go wrong in raising money; only a few go well. You can easily run afoul of the law, both state and federal, without realizing it. (Did you know that if you talk to as few as 35 people about purchasing stock in your venture, the Securities and Exchange Commission may interpret your activities as those of a "public" company upon which the full weight of federal regulation is brought to bear—an enormous expense to you!?!) If this is all new to you, you may want to get some help. Common sense is not a reliable guide.

TABLE 6-2: BUSINESS PLAN OUTLINE

   I.   Introduction
  II.   Description of the Product
 III.   Key Questions
        What is the magnitude of the market?
        What are the key competitors?
        What advantages does your product offer?
        What percent of the market can you expect to
           capture? Why?
        What will be your product lifetime? (How long will
           the market be there?)
        What are the market trends?
        What are cost versus sales projections?
 IV.   Development Plan
        How long will it take to develop the product?
        How much will it cost to develop the product?
           (Use PERT or critical path charts. Identify
           resources needed and cost projections.)
  V.   Production Plan
        How much will it cost to produce the product?
        How much time and labor will be required?
           (Show PERT or critical path chart; show cost
           and resource projections.)
 VI.   Management
        Include resumes of key people.
 VII.   Marketing Plan
        How do you plan to capture this market?
        What is the advertising strategy?
        How much will this strategy cost?
           (Normally marketing is about 10 percent
           of the selling price.)
VIII.   Support Plan
        How will you repair and maintain your product?
        (NOTE: the most common omission in a product
        business plan is the cost of repair parts and labor,
        and the maintenance of capital equipment used in
        production.)
 IX.   Financial Strategy
        How much start-up capital is needed?
        What will be the cash flow at each stage?

Where is the break-even point?
What are the end-point returns?
(Show three to five years projected financial
statements, profit and loss, and cash flow
projections.)

6.5 DEVELOPING YOUR PRODUCT

Product development is a complex art when it is undertaken
commercially. It is important to remember that the object of
the activity is not to make a single working piece of hardware,
but to create a body of special information that will allow
inexpensive production in large numbers. Moreover, the product
must suit the needs and wishes of an identifiable group of
potential buyers at a price they will be willing to pay. Just
because you think something is a great idea does not mean
someone else will.

The point of this activity is to gather all the information that
allows you to meet the specifications, or at least come close
enough to have commercial value. It is important to ferret out
all the details, all costs of hardware, expanded materials (molds?)
and processes. It is imperative that you record all this information in a clear and accessible form.

A consistently maintained notebook, with entries dated and
witnessed, can be an important part in establishing patent
protection. The product of development projects is *information*.
That's what you want to preserve and protect.

As an enthusiastic do-it-yourselfer you will want to control
your natural tendency to use your time expensively. For
example, we once spent $50 and a lot of time creating a printed
circuit board in the basement when a local PC board shop could
have done the job (better) from our existing artwork for $30.
Development programs call for sensible management if they are
to be cost effective.

6.6 UNDERWRITER'S LABORATORY APPROVAL

If your product involves line power (115 volts a.c.) or requires
modification of the power supply in equipment that uses line
power, you will need to get Underwriters' Laboratory approval.

This involves three costs:

1. The cost of their testing your product before production.
2. A manufacturing cost to UL on each product carrying the UL label.
3. An annual inspection charge.

If your product attaches to another product that already has UL approval, you must get a UL approval both for your product and for the combined product. Some parts and components of the product also need UL approval. Typical UL approval costs for a product in 1972 were $10,000 for a telephone modem using line power. Every change or modification you have made requires UL approval again.

You do not need UL approval for low-voltage products. Cards for the S-100 bus use low voltages and do not require UL approval. Rebuilding used Selectrics and adding interfaces to Selectrics for computers do not require UL approval if you use the same power supply and make no modifications. No washer or bushing can be changed. If your Selectric interface has its own power supply, you will need UL approval.

Note that UL is not the only organization with influence on the public release of your product; various county and state laws may apply. Check it out.

6.7 MARKETING YOUR PRODUCT

Once your prototype is operational, you are ready to market your product and start production. Both require capital, but now you have a marketable product that can be shown to any businessman who is interested. If you have anything in your product that is patentable, it would be wise to begin the patent process before showing the product to a venture capitalist.

Currently there is little control over the quality of products on the microcomputer market. In one product area, for example, there are manufacturers with very poor products and $45,000-a-year advertising budgets; they seem to be doing quite well in spite of their poor products. Some journals (such as *Dr. Dobb's*) refuse to sell advertising and are addressing this problem with critical (and good) reviews. Others will take any advertising with no product reviews. It is hard for a garage-shop operation to sell a good product against a poor product that has good advertising and media coverage.

If you must start small, concentrate on your local area. Offer your product on a consignment basis to local computer stores, being sure to tell the store enough about your product to make them interested in selling it. If your product is on consignment with a local store and they are not enthusiastic about selling it, either get them excited or withdraw your product from their store.

Selling hardware requires both time and work, so if you can't provide both, avoid this market. While your product is new you will find yourself investing a lot of time and money for very little return. If you get too many installation questions, rewrite your installation manual. If repair time is slowing you down, rewrite the diagnostics section of your manual. Above all, be enthusiastic about your product. Use your own system to explore new applications for your product.

If you plan to sell your product through computer stores, assume that the store will keep 30-50 percent of the retail price. Check the publications of Image Resource, 717 Lakefield Road, Suite B, Westlake Village, California 91361, for listings of stores. Retail stores are opening, closing, and changing hands with such rapidity that correct, up-to-date lists are not easy to maintain.

7 HOW TO SELL SYSTEMS AS A CONSULTANT

If you have the right kind of professional skills, you can make money selling systems. When you sell a system, you charge a retail markup plus a consulting fee and installation charge. It is a relatively easy business to get into and does not require a lot of capital. Further, it is not necessary to sell from a retail store; at least at the start you may want to operate from your home.

7.1 GETTING STARTED

The skills required are a good grounding in software, a reasonable knowledge of hardware, and some systems analysis experience. You should be able to develop complex business accounting packages; even if you buy the packages from someone else, you should be able to make alterations. If you are a professional programmer, you probably have the necessary software skills. Knowledge of computers clearly must be accompanied by some knowledge of accounting or other disciplines in which the computer will be used. You also must be able to install and service the hardware. Other than reading books or taking courses at a junior college, possibly the best way to learn about hardware is to take your system apart and experiment with it. One book we suggest for this is *8080 Microcomputer Experiments*, by Howard Boyet (dilithium Press, 1978). Another excellent book is, *The Systems Analyst: How to Design Computer-Based Systems*, by Jerry Atwood (Hayden Press, 1977). Other references are shown in Table 7-1.

TABLE 7-1: REFERENCES FOR COMPUTER CONSULTING

Brown, Leslie, *How to Start Your Own Systems House*, 2nd Edition, Essex Publishing Co., 285 Bloomfield Ave., Caldwell, NJ 07006, $36.

Handbook of Small Business Computer Consultants, Essex Publishing Co., 285 Bloomfield Ave., Caldwell NJ 07006, $28.

One of the best ways to get started in this business is to hold a Saturday workshop for businessmen in a local motel conference room. (Suggestions for marketing this workshop are in Chapter 10.) Your workshop should be tutorial rather than a sales pitch, directly addressing the needs of the businessman. Avoid "computer-ese," technical system specifications, and the history of the computer. Identify where the computer can help the businessman. Set up your demonstration system with plenty of business-oriented software such as payroll, general ledger, word processing and mailing list processors. Guide the businessman through the process of selecting his system. Illustrate different kinds of computer systems and how they relate to various kinds of applications. Show him what questions to ask and tell him what your system can do for him. Have samples of the printed outputs from the various programs and brochures available to take. Avoid any sales pitches or concentration of your time with any one person. Be sure to get a list of all attendees and notify them during the workshop that you will be calling on them to discuss their specific needs.

7.2 SYSTEM ANALYSIS AND FEASIBILITY STUDIES

On the initial contact with your client, carry no brochures or proposals. Investigate your client's needs and do a systems analysis. What are the desires, needs and objectives of the organization and of the people who will be using the system? Listen to the client's problem and discover what he needs and what he wants (these may not be the same!). You are not selling a computer; you are selling a solution to one or more problems. Get copies of any forms he may be using that will involve the computer application.

Your next step is a feasibility study. What are the economics and technical aspects of the application? Is the system economically feasible? Is the system technically feasible? Can it be economically operated? What is your client's financial credibility? What level of back-up is needed? What level of operator education is needed? What about data verification for accuracy?

7.3 THE SYSTEM DESIGN AND PROPOSAL

Now you can prepare a system design and proposal tailored to your client's specific application (Table 7-2). The proposal should detail the hardware and software you plan to deliver, what the system will do, the benefits and savings he can anticipate, the cost (including any furniture, cables, etc.), payment schedule, acceptance criteria, service and education you will provide, and any options available and their cost—and, most important—delivery time. A set of these requirements is shown in Table 7-3. Use your computer to set up, edit and print your proposal.

When you are ready to present your proposal, set up a definite appointment. You might want to get your proposal to the client ahead of time so that you can plan to close the sale at your meeting. Anticipate objections and have your answers ready. Be prepared to spend as much time as is needed. If you estimate that it will take you one hour to make your presentation, allow at least two hours to close the sale.

7.4 CLOSING THE SALE

Know your competitors. What are the specifications for the competitors products? What is the reliability factor? What is the delivery time? Does your system have any added software features? Your customer may want to comparison shop. If you can provide all the necessary comparisons, you may be able to close the sale on your first call.

The last, and perhaps the most important, part of closing the sale is determining how you are going to be paid. Standard business terms are net thirty days after delivery, but there are a variety of plans you can use. For instance, you can ask for 10 percent down, with the balance to be paid in three equal monthly payments over a 90-day period. Regardless of the

TABLE 7-2: SYSTEM IMPLEMENTATION FLOW DIAGRAM

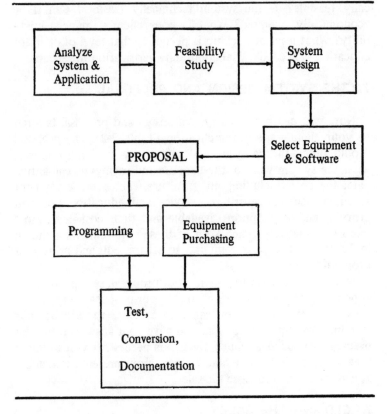

TABLE 7-3: ISSUES ADDRESSED BY THE PROPOSAL

1. Hardware and software to be delivered
2. Benefits and savings to be expected
3. Cost (include furniture, cables, etc.)
4. Payment method and schedule
5. Acceptance criteria
6. Service to be provided, warranty
7. Education to be provided
8. Options available and cost
9. Delivery time

terms you agree upon, they should be the same for everyone. You should not be too restrictive or you won't get very much business. Conversely, you should not be too open or you will have to carry a large accounts receivable. Businessmen inherently distrust anyone who expects full prepayment or cash on delivery. The only time you should ask for full payment or cash on delivery is when you feel the company is financially unsound.

7.5 INSTALLATION, DOCUMENTATION AND EDUCATION

Once the sale is closed, don't leave your customer hanging while you go after the next one. Get documentation to him and help him get started with facilities planning and programming. You can start his education while he waits for delivery. The more documentation you can provide, the fewer calls and questions you will get. If the customer does call, tell him where in the documentation he can find the answer so that he will get used to using the manuals for answers. If the equipment or software manuals are incomplete, add your own documentation. Tell him how much power he will need, what type of power, and the space needed.

After the equipment is installed, visit the site occasionally for questions the client may have. By staying sensitive to your customer's needs on a continuing basis, you will get repeat business as he expands.

8 HOW TO OPEN YOUR OWN COMPUTER STORE

One of the first computer stores was started in 1975 by Dick Heiser in West Los Angeles, with an initial investment of $15,000. Today you would need $100,000 or more to start a computer store, and you probably will be competing with several other local stores.

If you have the capital and are still interested, you will find that it will take at least two years to get the store in the black, and this will be two years of hard work. Are you and your family willing to forgo any vacations and other luxuries for the time it will take to get the store going?

At the start you will probably be the only employee. If you go from consulting to retailing, you will find you will be making only one-third to one-fourth as much per hour selling personal computers. You will need to be bookkeeper, carpenter, marketing director, systems analyst, salesman, public relations manager, personnel manager, technician, programmer, and purchasing director. If you are still interested, check with your local Small Business Administration office, and you will discover your odds for success are less than fifty-fifty.

Major causes of small business failures are the lack of or mismanagement of capital, the lack of an aggressive marketing program and poor accounting practices—in that order.

Why, then, would anyone want to start a store? Simple—the market is growing exponentially. In the Portland, Oregon, metropolitan area we have five computer stores and 25,000 small businesses that are potential customers. If the local stores sold a system a day, it would take eight years to saturate the local business market. This number does not include businesses with a single owner/employee, writers (who use word processors), artists, private accountants, private investment consultants, lawyers, doctors, dentists, real estate brokers or any of a host of other occupations. This also does not include larger corporations that could use several microprocessor systems.

8.1 THREE TYPES OF DEALERS

These markets can be addressed by three types of dealers. The first type is a small-volume dealer who works part-time at sales and depends on consulting and service to provide additional income. He generally does not have accounts receivable or much of an inventory. Therefore, he cannot expect the sales volume of larger stores.

The second type is the independent retailer. He has the greatest risk. He is into the business on a full-time basis and must compete not only with other independent stores, but with the franchise operations and company stores such as Radio Shack, DEC and IBM. Unless he can offer a strong service and product base, he will not be able to survive. Inventory is also a problem, as deliveries on many products can be three months or more.

A third type is the franchise operator. The risk here is much smaller (less than 10 percent fail), and the owner gets management and inventory support from a strong base.

If you choose to be a part-time dealer, you will still need to incorporate and establish a business name. You can afford to spend more time with your customers than a store or retail outlet can, but your customers will expect more specialized service. In some cases, this may involve special software or hardware. You also will need to offer maintenance and service support. Your price to the customer should include the equipment cost, any retail mark-up on the equipment and your system analyst fee, which can be 15 percent or more.

Some suppliers may not wish to sell to you as a part-time dealer. If another full-time store in your city is selling the supplier's product, the supplier often wishes to protect his dealer and will not sell to another dealer in the same city. If you experience this problem, move on to another supplier. You should find good suppliers for the more common products, such as memory boards and control processors. You can purchase other products for your customers at the retail cost, and if your business is good, you might be able to work a discount with your local retail outlet.

Systems can be purchased for resale in single-unit quantities at a discount of 20-25 percent from system distributors who buy in quantity. Microage (1425 W. 112th Place #101, Tempe, AZ 85281) is perhaps the largest and best known. Two others are Computer Systems Distributors, Inc. (3470 Erie Blvd. East, Syracuse, NY 13214), and Marketline Systems, Inc. (2337 Philmont Ave., Huntington Valley, PA 19006). In contacting these distributors, ask for their OEM buying plan.

Inventory will be a problem. If you are starting with a minimum of capital, sell your first systems to businessmen you know and trust, offering them a discount for waiting until the order has been delivered. This will keep your capital outlay to a minimum. Once the capital is built up, invest in the equipment that is reliable, has good delivery time, and can be sold quickly. Use these rules consistently to control your inventory.

The franchise operation is another option for retail sales. Several franchise chains are already operating (Table 8-1), and the number is expected to grow. Some specialize with a single manufacturer (such as the Altair Computer Centers); others support several suppliers (such as Byte). The initial investment required is about $100,000 for most franchisers. The franchise store may have the advantage of a stronger inventory base than the independent dealer, better management support, and qualified people who can help you get your store going with a minimum of mistakes. In exchange, they get a percentage of your sales—generally 8 percent.

If you are serious about being part of a franchise operation, call the company and get initial particulars; not all are reliable. Paul Conover's article in *Personal Computing* (September/October 1977) lists over four dozen questions you should ask the franchiser. A safe bet is to concentrate on operation headquarters in California, since that state has very strict rules controlling franchise operations. So if the franchise is registered in California, you can expect good support.

Some franchises will open only one store in an area, and your area already may have a store in operation or one that is planned. Ask for a "disclosure" from the franchiser that gives full details on the terms and conditions of the offering, reading it carefully before signing anything. Normally, a deposit is required; this gives you a period of several months to raise the additional capital and locate a site. We also would strongly advise visiting the franchiser personally and resolving questions on their location. Check their inventory and management and visit at least one of their stores to get the view of their operation from a store owner.

The second alternative, the independent store owner, is dependent upon his relationship with his own customers for his advertisement. He will be competing with franchise operations and (soon) IBM, Texas Instruments, and DEC for customers. His service and inventory may be just as good, but he is at a disadvantage is marketing. Most of the independent stores that are successful got into the business early and know as much about running computer retail stores as some of the franchise operations. If you plan to start this type of store, you should have had some level of business experience. Some of the questions you will need to resolve are shown in Table 8-2. Visit stores and imitate successful ones. Your local Small Business Administration Office can also help with literature, programs, and other assistance.

You may want to join the Computer Retailer's Association. This is a well-organized group that has plenty of experience in making the computer store work. For information, contact Portia Isaacson, EDS, 7171 Forest Lane, Dallas, Texas. You should also obtain as many of the published resources as possible, including the magazines published exclusively for dealers (see Table 8-3). Join area organizations for retailers, such as the Western Computer Dealer Association and the South California Dealer Association.

8.2 SELECTING EQUIPMENT

Select with care the equipment you will be selling, and give good service support for each product. If you sell too many types of equipment, your service support will be spread too thinly and you will not be able to give good, professional service. Limit yourself to about three system manufacturers. The application markets for these systems should be different, thus minimizing the capital required. Classify into market groups the systems you could possibly sell, choosing only one system from each group, for a maximum of three systems. An example might be the Apple, Cromemco, and Data General.

TABLE 8-1: FRANCHISE OPERATIONS

Altair Computer Centers

Pertec Computer Corporation
20630 Nordoff Street
Chatsworth, CA 91311

BYTE
930 West Maude Avenue
Sunnyvale, CA 94086

Computerland
1922 Republic Avenue
San Leandro, CA 94577

TABLE 8-2: Questions To Resolve in Opening a Store

What service contracts will you provide?
What warranty will you provide with your kits?
What warranty will you provide with other products?
How much will you charge for service?
How much will you charge for systems analysis?
How will you handle repair of mechanical equipment, as in
    floppy disk drives?
Will you do contract programming?
How many books and magazines will you stock? What type?
What manufacturers will you support?

Maintain good stock control. Use your computer to monitor inventory on a daily basis. Over 90 percent of small business theft is by employees. If it takes you months to discover a loss, you could lose your shirt without knowing it. Survey some computer stores in your area and get information on the level of security needed. Good stock control also helps you identify the products that move well so that you can keep these in stock.

At least one computer store in the Portland area is already using the computers he sells to do his own accounts receivable, accounts payable, general ledger and inventory. As a result, he has gained insights on business problems that the other stores haven't, and he is selling most of the business systems in our area.

TABLE 8-3: DEALER RESOURCES

Computer Dealer Magazine (free to qualified dealers), Gordon Publications, P.O.Box 2106-R, Morristown, NJ 07960

How to Start a Computer Store and Keep it Running, $200, from Audio Visual Department, CCM, Inc., P.O.Box 7343, Oakland, CA 94601, (415-530-7312)

1977 Computer Store Survey, $295, Image Resources, 717 Lakefield Road, Suite B, Westlake Village, CA 91361, (805-494-6277)

MediaSCOPE, 1001 East Touhy Ave., Suite 112, Des Plaines, IL 60618 (Midwest area only)

Computer Retailing (free to dealers), 1760 Peachtree Road, N. W., Atlanta, GA 30357

How to Convert a Hobby Store into a Million-dollar Business Equipment Store, $189, Image Resource, 717 Lakefield Road, Suite B, Westlake Village, CA 91361

How to Start a Successful Computer Store, $38, from Essex Publishing Co., 285 Bloomfield Ave., Caldwell, NJ 07008

8.3 MARKETING IDEAS FOR STORES

Your store will create an image to the public. What image design to you wish to create? A store name of "Business Computers, Inc." will immediately identify to the passing motorist that it is after the business market. The name "Computerworld" leaves anyone passing to make his own assumptions. Your window displays, name, and store design should always image your store to the type of customer you wish to attract. Your window displays also should tell a story.

The store layout properly should segregate your service, sales, demonstration, and magazine areas, establishing a traffic pattern for these areas. Fast-moving inventory (books, magazines, media supplies) should be at the back of the store, forcing customers to walk by your more expensive products with each visit. Learn some things from your neighborhood grocer: he puts the milk and eggs at the back of the store! Change displays often—fast product turnover is important. Don't be afraid to mark down products that are not moving.

Use advertising in the Yellow Pages and local newspapers. In the Yellow Pages, put a small advertisement under several headings. In the newspaper, use small advertisements, repeating them often.

Remember that your best advertisements are your satisfied customers. Get your customer's name and remember it. Use it several times before she or he leaves the store, and teach your employees to do the same.

9 HOW TO HOLD A LOCAL OR REGIONAL COMPUTER SHOW

Everyone knows about the big computer shows in Los Angeles, San Francisco and Chicago—but what about a show in your own home town? In many cities (as in Houston and Trenton), local computer enthusiasts have gotten together and created their own faire. If you live in a metropolitan area, chances are you can put together a computer show with the help of a few friends such as members of your local computer club. You all might earn some money in the process, although you probably will not make too much, and the planning can be very time consuming. Are you willing to do the work? If you are, there are other benefits that cannot be measured in strict monetary terms. For instance, you will probably build up a good sense of community among those who work with you. And if your local computer club is involved in the show, you can gain a lot of new members. The local contacts you make will be good for your own business (system sales, consulting or whatever), and you will develop a valuable mailing list. You also will learn a lot about the computer business in general.

9.1 THE FIRST PLANNING MEETING

You should start planning your show at least a year ahead of time. It will take you at least this long to sell the idea, raise the capital, pull together your exhibitors, establish a program, and properly market the faire.

Your first job is to establish a pilot committee. The show will take work—lots of it—and no one in your committee should be there with any false ideas about the amount of work involved.

At least two types of personalities should be represented on the committee:

1. One or more people with extensive contacts in the computer industry and an understanding of the industry.
2. Someone competent in advertising, selling and communications.

Start your planning sessions at a location that is convenient for everyone involved. Outline your agenda ahead of time and deal with only a few key items on the agenda; i.e., don't plan your program or brainstorm on detail issues at this time. Assign someone to take minutes and keep a record of decisions. Typical agenda items can include:

1. How are you going to get resource capital?
2. What market do you intend to reach?
3. What committees will you need and what will be their responsibilities?

You will need resource capital just to get started, one of the major reasons faires have failed has been undercapitalization. You will need money to reserve a facility, as well as to advertise and market your faire. If you don't have the cash, put together a prospectus or proposal and go after the money. This means that much of your planning should be done before you begin to seek out funds. For money, look to local computer stores, as well as your computer club, pooling resources if necessary. Some cash will be flowing in as exhibitors reserve booths, but you will need some capital to get things going. Many exhibitors will not reserve booths until they have already seen aggressive marketing of the faire.

You must also define your intended markets early in your planning. Typical markets might include engineers, businessmen, educators, hobbyists, and data processing executives.

In addition to the pilot or steering committee, your working committees might include:

1. Advertising—responsible for advertising and promotion aspects of the faire.
2. Exhibitor—responsible to attracting as many exhibitors as possible. (Sales, sales, sales, without which, failure.)
3. Program—responsible for planning the program—speakers, banquets, special attractions.

4. Facilities—responsible for such facilities planning as space utilization, food, lounge areas, message centers and such.

If your steering committee is large enough, its members might be the leaders of the individual committees. You also will need someone or a committee to keep track of finances.

9.2 THE CREATIVITY BEGINS

Your committee heads now can build their committees from local and regional people and hold some committee meetings. Meanwhile, you've got some work to do.

Begin building an outline for a prospectus or proposal on your faire project. If you plan to go after venture capital, this will be a necessity. Even if you already have the assets to get the faire going, it's still a good idea to put together a prospectus.

You will need some "market research" on what goes into a successful show and what it takes to turn a profit. Several local shows, such as the Houston show and the Trenton Computer Festival, have done well. Contact the successful people involved in these shows and learn from them. Define your goals clearly and the methods of evaluating your progress. Set up your time schedules, budgets and organizational structure. Maintain contact with your committee chairmen, motivating and keeping the idea moving. Look at the ideas for the business plan in Chapter 6 and the appendix on proposal writing. Use these outlines to build your own. "Flesh out" the final copy, using your computer as a word processor. This will give you a lot of flexibility in altering sections as your committees do their work.

Call your second steering committee meeting after the committees are organized and operating. Count on having a steering committee meeting anytime you recognize major problems.

9.3 GETTING THE EXHIBITORS—THE EXHIBITORS COMMITTEE

Your exhibitors are the primary source of your income for the faire. Start early with some aggressive marketing to get these exhibitors, and set target goals for how many you want.

Allow for plenty of exhibit categories, such as microbooths for low-budget small businesses and home-brew exhibitors. You might even allow an exhibitor a free booth if the exhibit is clearly non-commercial and will draw big crowds. It is important, however, to have a firm, well-defined policy for exhibitors. There should not be one type of policy for one exhibitor and another policy for someone else. Establish revenue from your exhibits based on your projected costs.

Build up a mailing list of all possible exhibitors in your town and put this on your computer in a mailing list program. These could include electronic parts suppliers, office supply stores (who sell media supplies), local computer media suppliers, retail computer stores, and regional representatives for larger companies such as Wang, Univac, IBM and DEC. Code each address by the type of business so that, as reservations for booths are mailed in, you can see what types of businesses are reserving space and the status of each reservation. This helps you to concentrate your advertising on the markets that are responding and to identify your weaker markets so you can replan your advertising strategy to these markets. Start a bulk mailing to all possible exhibitors telling them why they should exhibit in your faire. Use repeat mailings with the cost of each as low as possible. Keep your market definition for the show in mind as you contact exhibitors.

Avoid the larger non-local manufacturers. Most are overloaded with show requests and only exhibit at large shows. Work through your local retail stores instead. Often a manufacturer will have high-quality displays for use in national shows that can be loaned to local shows.

Some of your exhibitors might find that planning a booth is a new experience for them, and they may need help in making their booths economically successful. A short newsletter or brochure in your mailing with some helpful ideas might stimulate more ideas on their part and might mean the difference on their decision as to whether to man a booth.

As the time for your faire approaches, you will need to work closely with the facilities committee on getting the exhibits into the faire, insuring security and getting them out after the faire is over. Many facilities require any exhibit construction on the show site to be done by union employees—even if this means hammering a nail in place. If the union charge is $40 an hour with a minimum of $40, that nail could be expensive. Check into all the rules and regulations, let your exhibitors know what they are, and be prepared to help your exhibitors avoid as much of this expense as possible.

9.4 PLANNING THE PROGRAM—THE PROGRAM COMMITTEE

Design your show so that it will have a festive flair with plenty of excitement, color and entertainment. Offer something for everyone—tease all your markets with some aspect of the show.

As you plan the major part of your program, build it around the market you are trying to attract. Provide speakers, presentations and special features to address the needs of this specific market.

If you are attracting the hobbyist market, you can use features such as robots, computerized portrait photographs, music synthesizers, computer art, contests, biorhythms, and science fiction films. You might want to expand this market base by combining your show with an amateur radio convention or a Star Trek convention. Try to touch as many senses as possible—sight, sound, taste. Use plenty of games and simulations. Draw your speakers primarily from your local area and emphasize tutorial aspects. You might want at least one "name" speaker from outside your area who is well known as a draw. Sessions should be free or very low in cost.

If you are attracting the business market, you will need good speeches by qualified leaders in the computer industry. Businessmen are not interested in games and biorhythms. They are looking at the bottom line and want to know how to purchase a system and make money with it. They are willing to pay $10 or $20 a session for hard answers they can use. They will ask questions about accounting software, inventory control and mailing list processing. Businessmen want to know how to evaluate hardware and software. Plan good in-depth sessions with good leadership. Fly in talent you do not have locally.

Some faires advertise for speakers and permit almost anyone with an interesting topic to speak at one of the sessions. Topical sessions are planned involving the speakers that respond. Speakers are paid nothing, but are given a faire pass and a copy of the proceedings. Others faires address specific interests and invite well-known speakers to address these interests. The speakers are paid well, and those that attend the faire pay a high admission cost to offset the costs of bringing these speakers in. Communicate with each speaker ahead of time. Send them their admission pass and a copy of the program.

Banquets generally are losers at faires, but whether to have one or not is a decision to make early in the process. If you plan to have a banquet, it will require its own program and planning committee. If planned properly, it can still show a modest profit.

One interesting idea used in many programs is to set up large-screen television projections to illustrate video displays in the sessions. The typical PET computers can drive the video directly, producing a display every one can see. You may want to rent one of these for the duration of the faire.

Evaluation of the program is important to help you plan the next faire. One idea would be to have a drawing using the returned evaluations forms. A few prizes can enhance the excitement.

9.5 MARKETING AND ADVERTISING YOUR SHOW— THE ADVERTISING COMMITTEE

Advertising is the primary key to the success of your show. Where you advertise, when you advertise and how you advertise are all critical. Study the marketing guidelines in Chapter 10 and build a strategy on this.

When you advertise your show, direct your message to those you expect to attend. Use newspapers, posters in local stores, word of mouth, and direct mail. Mailing lists for businessmen can generally be purchased through the local Chamber of Commerce. These lists usually can be profiled to the type of businesses you want to attract. Newspaper coverage should be limited to the business section, the entertainment section, or the Sunday supplement section the week or so before the faire. Television coverage is too expensive, but do invite television reporters to the faire to encourage them to get material for their news programs. Notify all the computer magazines, and check into locally published magazines.

To save registration time, use your advertising to sell registration tickets. You also can sell tickets through retail stores and the club, thus minimizing the lines on Saturday morning as your 5,000 attendees try to get into the show!

Your sales people should project a good image. They should be excited about the faire, be well-informed, and communicate well. It also helps if they know the market to which they are selling; i.e., a businessman can sell a faire to a businessman easier than a hobbyist can.

9.6 THE FINANCIAL ASPECT

Your project should have a well-defined budget, and the financial status should be continually monitored against this budget. A microcomputer system can give you this information on a daily basis; a good accounting system can generate all the reports and give you a continuing report of your financial status.

There are no special rules for how much to charge for exhibits, sessions, or admissions; this is something you will have to decide. It would be quite easy, however, to write a short program to simulate your income. Input variables would be the number of each type of booth, the rental, the admission cost, and expected attendance. If sessions have special prices, you also will need to include these and their expected attendance. The computer can then project your income, and you can compare this income with your budget. Variables can be altered easily for new calculations.

9.7 FACILITIES PLANNING—THE FACILITIES COMMITTEE

Your first assignment will be to find a location for the faire. Other concerns involve lodging, food, and transportation.

Begin with a survey of all possible facilities in your area, including coliseums, auditoriums, science museums, hotels, motels, and college campuses. Find out where the space is available, how appropriate it is (can exhibits be moved in and out easily?), union rates, and costs. You might also check with groups who have used the facilities. What problems did they discover? Check into lodging, food, and transportation at each facility; then make your decision.

Expect most of those attending to be from the local area. You will need good lodging and food for out-of-town speakers and attendees, so try to set up one hotel as the official conference hotel. You should be able to obtain a flat rate. To find out what each hotel (or motel) has to offer, talk to the sales manager.

Once the basic location has been picked, notify the advertising committee so they can get the advertising moving. This should be at least six months before the show, and preferably earlier. Now begin planning your lodging, transportation, and food. A local travel agency might be able to help you set up some transportation packages. Also, check with the buses and trains. Most people won't be traveling far, and the novelty of doing something special with other computer friends might be interesting.

At the time for the faire approaches, there will be plenty of details:

1. Work with the program committee for speaker facilities, taping, audio-visual equipment, and PA systems.
2. Plan a message center so that attendees can be notified in an emergency.
3. Plan a lounge area for informal discussions with salesmen and customers.
4. How about some fast-food counters for quick lunches and coffee breaks? Plan for variety, quality and low cost.
5. How do you plan to insure the security of the exhibits?

9.8 SHOW TIME

During the show you will have the real test of your leadership. Dozens of problems will need decisions, and you will find yourself quite busy. Expect Murphy's law—if anything can go wrong, it will! Keep back-up equipment and contingency plans available at all times.

10 HOW TO MARKET YOUR PRODUCT OR SERVICE

Marketing your product or service involves two aspects: surveying and selling. Marketing is easily one of the two most critical aspects in the success of your business (the second is good financial management). For this reason, you should expect successful marketing to involve a lot of creativity and financial resources, as well as a well-developed strategy.

10.1 SURVEYING

The surveying aspect of your marketing program actually should begin before you develop your product. It should be initiated into your business whenever:

1. You plan a new product or your sales are below expectations, or
2. You find dissatisfied customers (with your product or a competitor's), or
3. You plan to improve an old product.

The survey can be done informally (as at computer faires) or in a more formal, planned strategy. It also can be done face to face, by mail, or by telephone. Surveys vary in methods, styles, and approaches.

1. You can survey users of a particular class of products (as printers) or user's of a particular application (as word processors) to determine whether they are happy or unhappy or have needs not being met.
2. You can survey current vendors to determine what needs they address and what products are available. This involves

studying magazine advertisements and brochures. How is the product sold? What selling strategies appear to work?

3. You can do a study of marketing strategies. Are products of the type you are offering generally sold by dealerships or by mail order? Who buys this type of product? Why do you think they buy the product (what was their need)? Would your product be more popular in a particular geographic area? Why?

4. What is the attitude of your market? Attitudes are critical in determining how to relate your product to the need. A customer who is afraid of technology or knows nothing of even the simplest of computer languages might be afraid to purchase a microcomputer system. Evaluation of attitudes is difficult, as users generally will not admit their fears, ignorance or prejudices. Attitude evaluation usually must be done indirectly or by analysis of purchasing patterns. Analyzing users for reasons they purchased systems, for example, will also tell you their attitudes.

5. You can do a market potential study. How many small businesses are there in your city? What kinds of businesses are they?

Many companies specialize in market analysis, but for most applications you can do your own surveying very successfully. The survey should attempt to answer the following questions:

1. How should my product or service be marketed (face to face, mail order, dealerships, computer faires, etc.)?
2. What is a fair market price?
3. What are the needs of the market and how does my product relate to these needs?
4. Who will be buying my product? What is his or her background (experience, educational level, etc.)?
5. How much should I spend on advertising?
6. To whom should I address the advertising?
7. Where should I do my advertising?
8. How large is my market?
9. Will this market respond to direct mail?
10. Can I close some sales by telephone?

Market surveys need not be expensive or time consuming. Often your data can be obtained for a low cost or even free from your bank, the government, the Small Business Administration, or universities. An excellent resource for information on how to do low-cost market surveys is Don Dible's *The Pure Joy of Making More Money* ($10 from the Entrepreneur Press, 3422 Astoria Circle, Fairfield, CA 94533). Use your computer to reduce and analyze the data.

10.2 THE ESSENCE OF ADVERTISING

Remember that most people today are information overloaded. How much of your mail do you read? How many of the advertisements in a computer magazine do you read? What determines which advertisements you read? *You read advertisements that relate directly to your needs*!

Try an experiment: scan through the last issue of your favorite computer magazine, then close the magazine and write down the advertisements you remember. Then open the magazine and study these advertisements; why did they capture your attention? To what particular need did the advertiser relate his product? The computer is a direction, not an objective. The advertiser sells a solution to a problem, not a computer. Here are a few of the more common needs:

survival	romance
security	adventure
fame	health
power and control	popularity
making money	

What others can you add to the list? Classify each of the advertisements from your magazine relative to the need to which the product is related. The advertisement relates the product to the need and then calls for action.

An excellent text for marketing skills is Philip Kotler's *Marketing for Nonprofit Organizations* (Prentice-Hall, 1975).

10.3 DIRECT SALES

The fastest way to sell anything is face to face. If you want to be successful, you must spend part of your time selling. Salesmanship is a learned skill which anyone can acquire. It is something you do every day in one way or another. Any time you try to convince another person of something, you are selling. You can increase your business enormously by learning a few basic sales techniques.

Starting at the beginning, let's clear up a common misconception. There is no such thing as a "natural-born salesman." In reality, any average person interested in selling can learn to be a good salesman. The glib salesman who talks around issues is quite likely to lose orders to the person who is technically competent and can demonstrate the worth and application of the product.

Buyers today favor the salesman from whom they can buy most profitably. The era of the salesman who went about handing out expensive cigars, slapping people on the back and telling jokes is gone. Buyers are still human and susceptible to attention and flattery, but the emphasis is on business. The two most important qualities for being a good salesman are technical competence and honesty.

Assuming you already have the two most important qualities, let's concentrate on some of the lesser qualities, starting with the approach. The better informed you are about your prospect and his needs, the better your presentation will be. You can get most of what you need from the prospect when you speak to him—*but don't*! This interview is for selling, not research. If you are calling on a business rather than on an individual, here are some facts you should know:

1. What does his company do? If it is a computer store, what is the emphasis (e.g., to sell hardware, develop systems)?
2. What types of products/services can you sell him?
3. Is the company growing?
4. Does the company have good credit?
5. Who is the right person to contact?

Once you have this information, you are ready to set up the interview, working by appointment whenever possible. There are some simple rules to follow that will make your interviews more profitable. First, remember that it is up to you to get the interview. You are not entitled to someone's attention just because you can provide some benefit. Second, be sure you are seeing the right person. Finally, sell the interview before you sell your product. Normally, you should set up your appointment by telephone, techniques for which are covered in Section 10.4. You can also set up appointments by mail, but it is more time consuming.

There are as many ways to handle the interview as there are people who sell, but only a few people make very good presentations. When you make a presentation, you are trying to accomplish five things:

1. Hold the prospect's interest during the entire interview.
2. Clearly explain what you are selling and what benefits your prospect will derive from the purchase of your product.
3. Overcome or answer all your prospect's questions and objections.
4. Establish a need.
5. Make the prospect decide that he wants to buy. The greatest compliment paid to a salesman is, "Oh, the salesman didn't talk me into buying that product; I decided on my own."

Every good sales presentation is made up of five distinct phases:

Opening
Interest arousal
Presentation of benefits
Substantiation/verification of benefits
Closing

Entire books have been written on each of these steps, so our discussion of them will be brief.

As soon as you have properly introduced yourself, you must get the immediate and complete attention of your prospect. You can get his attention using an opening remark describing a benefit or setting the stage for some action. Let's look at some examples of handling this all-important first phase of the interview, the opening. The prospect wants to hear of the benefits directly applicable to his situation. A good opening remark should include a benefit the prospect wants, and your claim to that benefit must be thoroughly substantiated in the balance of your presentation. It must be something you can deliver, and it should be specific. For example, you might say, "Mr. Jones, I want to show you a computer system that will save you $10,000 a year." You can create the effect by using an anecdote, asking a thought-provoking question, or with a brief demonstration. Whatever you use, it should be attention getting, comfortable for you, and short.

With the prospect's attention in hand, you need to turn that attention into interest. You do this by telling him what specific benefits he will gain by using your product or service. These benefits should be laid out carefully so you can zero in on the ones he considers important.

Making the prospect want your product or service narrows the gap between more interest and a firm order. While interest is mainly a mental state, desire is an emotional state. Once someone decides he wants something, your only job is to show him how to buy it. People want whatever satisfies a strong need or gratifies a personal buying motive. People buy because they want a specific benefit. The ten most common "wants" are:

1. Wealth (e.g., increased profits)
2. Health
3. Admiration (e.g., pride and prestige)
4. Gratification
5. Amusement
6. Safety or security
7. Self-improvement
8. Time savings
9. Comfort
10. Functional value inherent in the product (e.g., you buy a car because it is a means of transportation)

Your product will probably appeal to not more than two of these wants. In order to sell your product, you must determine what these wants are, then convince the prospect you can fulfill them. The most important element of a convincing sales presentation is evident (substantiation of benefits). You can present this with a demonstration, visual aids, and facts and figures. The greatest presentation in the world won't sell anything if you don't have the facts to back it up. Making a prospect believe in your product or service depends on how well you support your statements. Even a demonstration isn't fully convincing without the facts that substantiate and explain.

The greatest presentation in the world is meaningless without a good close. Here are six ways to close a sale; try all of them, and then settle on two or three that work best for you.

1. Assume the prospect is going to buy. The assumptive close should never seem like a sales technique. You are merely going along with the prospect on a decision that has already been made. You start writing up the order and asking questions. If he doesn't stop you, he'll probably buy.
2. Get the prospect to agree on a minor point. For instance, you might ask a potential exhibitor at your computer show, "What color draping would you like for the booth?"

3. Offer the prospect something for buying now. "If you buy this system right now, I'll deliver it tomorrow and give you $100 off the price."
4. Give the prospect a reason to buy now. "We are going to increase the price of this system next month."
5. Make up a benefit and objection list. Drawing a line down the middle of a paper, label the left side "Benefits" and the right side "Objections." Have the customer fill out this sheet, starting with the benefits side, helping him as much as possible. When he has completed the benefits list, tell him to write down his objections. Smile pleasantly as you let him complete the right side alone.
6. Ask for the order. This seems obvious, but surprisingly few people remember to do it.

10.4 TELEPHONE SALES

The telephone can be one of your most important sales aids if you use it properly. However, it has two serious drawbacks: it is easier for people to say "no," and it denies you the give-and-take aspect of an interpersonal relationship. You should use the phone primarily for taking reorders, gathering information and setting up appointments. The techniques are essentially the same in all three instances, so we'll concentrate on the most important: setting up appointments.

Carefully plan what you are going to say and how you are going to say it. Write it down and practice it a few times before making your first call. You should try to condense all the pertinent information into a one-minute speech.

Start the conversation by identifying yourself, then tell the prospect why he would benefit from seeing you and ask for an appointment to explain these benefits. You will have little time to waste, so get right down to business. The whole purpose of your call is to make the prospect curious enough to give you an interview.

Be strictly low pressure when you call. Use a few words to assure your prospect that the interview will only take a few minutes of his valuable time and that he is under no obligation to buy. Just as appearance and other personal details are important in the actual interview, the personal impression you make over the phone is important. Here are ten rules for good phone salesmanship:

1. Speak distinctly and loudly enough to be heard.
2. Use a conversational tone (no evangelism).
3. Think and sound cheerful. An aid in this is to set a small mirror where you can look into it as you speak on the phone. If you are looking at an unsmiling face, perk up; it will add cheer to your voice.
4. Relax and enjoy yourself.
5. Keep you mouth close enough to the mouthpiece (without actually eating it, however).
6. Don't smoke, drink, or chew while on the phone.
7. Hold the phone with your hand, not with your shoulder.
8. Eliminate as much background noise as possible.
9. Give your prospect your undivided attention, both when you are talking and when you are listening.
10. Hang up the receiver gently.

10.5 WRITING COPY THAT SELLS

There is an old phrase in selling that is particularly apt to copywriting: "Tell them what you are going to tell them, tell them, tell them what you told them." It is perhaps the best advice anyone can give you. The primary thing we would like to add is: keep it short.

Before writing any kind of copy, ask yourself these three questions:

1. Who will buy my product or service?
2. Why will they buy it?
3. What benefits will they get from it?

Once you have answered all three of these questions in depth, you are ready to start thinking about your copy. Start by writing out a short description of your product or service. Then make an outline. You should do these initial steps regardless of the length of the material—it is just as important for a short piece as it is for a long one. Refer to the description and the outline often as you prepare the material.

Benefits, presented honestly, from a positive viewpoint, and in the prospect's language, still can fail to come through if you don't use the right words. The headline and the first sentence are the most critical spots. The words must be correct in these two places or the reader will not read any further. The two most powerful words you can use in a headline are: free and new. Variations of these two words also can be used, and the following words and phrases are natural attention getters:

money	sensational
just arrived	just released
newly discovered	coming
revolutionary	magic
urgent	miracle
announcing	easy
introducing	quick
now	startling
important	save
here	now
at last	see
improvement	remarkable
how to	love
hate	you can
fear	envy
mother	child
friend	make
you	your

Writing good copy is a creative undertaking, but there are some guidelines you can follow. A sales letter or an advertisement should have one, and only one, big idea. Copy without a central theme will fail to capture either the reader's imagination or attention.

Your copy must be logically organized. Each paragraph must lead to the next, going from support of your opening to the importance of immediate action.

Use short words, short sentences, and short paragraphs. Make the entire letter or ad only long enough to tell your story. Use a direct approach that clearly explains what you are trying to sell: Successful copy is usually single minded, simple, and crystal clear.

10.6 THE NEWS RELEASE

Take advantage of any free advertising you can get. Most computer magazines will give you a little free publicity on a new product if you send them a news release. This involves very little cost on your part and will help to get the product moving. Do not, however, expect to make enough money to purchase advertising from the response to the news release. With most magazines it will take three months from the time you mail the release to see it in print. If you wait this long to begin seeing returns on your investment, your first purchased advertisement will appear six months from when you mailed the news release. Your competitor will be well ahead of you.

Write your release as you wish to see it printed, as most editors will have little time to rewrite it. It should not be too long but should give enough information to help a reader make the decision to ask for more information. Use 8½×11- inch white bond paper. Use the title "NEWS RELEASE" in the upper left corner of the paper, and put "FOR IMMEDIATE RELEASE" under the larger title. Put your name, your company and your company's address (with phone number) in the upper right corner. Use double spacing for the copy (see Table 10-1). Add a "# # #" at the bottom of the release. The release may be more than a page, but it should be direct and not wordy. Be sure to put a date on the release.

If possible, send a photograph along with the news release. It should be a glossy black-and-white, at least 5″ × 7″, and preferably 8″ × 10″. Label the photograph on the reverse side using a felt marker, and include your name, company, and address. The photograph should also relate to the need; for example, if you are selling a mailing list program, show the printer printing a mailing list label. (It may seem obvious, but don't fold a photograph for mailing. People actually do that. It is an unwise practice; make sure that the kid you have stuffing envelopes knows it is unwise.)

Using Appendix B, send the release to all the computer magazines. Do not be afraid to try even the largest ones. A chance mention of our product by an editor in one large magazine earned us $1,000 in sales.

Send a cover letter with your release and ask for a rate card if you plan to purchase advertising. Use your computer to type letters and to address them. Be sure to include your product price in the release. When writing news releases to dealership magazines such as *Computer Retailing* and *Computer Dealer*, you should also include the dealer price. The dealer should expect to keep 40 percent of a book sale and about 20-30 percent on a hardware sale.

It normally takes about three months before the release will appear in print. The exception is *On-Line*, which, on occasion,

TABLE 10-1: SAMPLE NEWS RELEASE

Center for the Study of the Future
4110 N. E. Alameda
Portland, OR 97212
503-282-5835

October 10, 1979

NEWS RELEASE!

FOR IMMEDIATE RELEASE

MAILOUT mailing list processor now includes seven modules: BUILD, SORT, LIST, UPDATE, EXTRACT, LETTER, and HELP. Sorts on zip or address/title. Merges or extracts sub-files based on codes stored with address. Prints envelopes or labels in one or more columns. Processes letters against mailing lists. Label size is under user control. Send $5 for user's manual or $75 for complete program. Available in Commercial BASIC or Microsoft BASIC versions. Supplied on CP/M-type diskette. Dealer licenses available. Center for the Study of the Future, 4110 N. E. Alameda, Portland OR, 97212, (503) 282-5835.

###

---

can generate response in as little time as one week. Their newsletter is sent first class every three weeks.

Most magazines will publish your release with a bingo number, and you will receive computer-generated printouts of possible customers. Mail your brochures to each as quickly as possible.

There are other possibilities for free or low-cost advertising after the initial news release. One possibility would be to write a short article of interest on the application of your product. If you wish a quick response, offer this article free to anyone sending a self-addressed, stamped envelope. Send notices about the article to the magazines and quick-print the article at a local print shop. If response time is not a big factor, submit the article to a magazine for publishing.

10.7 THE BROCHURE

Your brochure is the primary marketing link between you and your customers. It should be designed to catch your customers' attention by identifying a need, relating your product to this need, and calling for action (see Table 10-2 and 10-3).

You should check with your local post office before designing your brochure. If you plan to mail the brochure, you will need to be aware of their regulations when you design it. These regulations will depend on how your corporation is established (profit, nonprofit, etc.). Ask the post office for two free brochures, one of which is entitled "Mailing Permits," and the other, "Mailer's Guide."

TABLE 10-2: Example of Poor Product Specification

SELECT SELECTRIC PRINTERS

* ASCII CODING AT 150 BAUD, RS-232
* RE-CONDITIONED HEAVY-DUTY SELECTRIC MECHANISM
* CLOSED-LOOP OPERATION CAPABILITY
* ELECTRONICS INCLUDES GOOD GROUND PLANE
    CONSTRUCTION TO MINIMIZE NOISE AND GOLD-PLATED
    PRINTED CIRCUIT BOARD CONTACTS
* ALL POWER SUPPLIES, EPROM AND ELECTRONICS INCLUDED
* WESTERN ELECTRIC BLUE TEXTURED FINISH
* ONLY $1,200

Order C.O.D from the Center for the Study of the Future, 4110 N. E. Alameda, Portland, OR 97212, (503) 282-5835.

You can design your brochure yourself, but the final copy you make for the printer should be camera ready. Use rub-on letters for lettering, available at many office supply stores. You can draw lines on the brochures with a light blue pencil which will not print on the final copy. It is best to use a non-reproducing blue pencil that is specifically designed for this. For diagrams, use a drawing pen and India ink. If any of the brochure is typed, use a carbon ribbon—not a cloth ribbon. Some general rules for the brochure design are shown in Table 10-4.

TABLE 10-3: Example of Good Product Specification

SELECT SELECTRIC PRINTERS

* IMPACT PRINTER FOR CRISP, CLEAR COPIES!
* MULTIPLE-COPY CAPABILITY!
* FIFTEEN CHARACTERS PER SECOND!
* INTERCHANGEABLE ELEMENTS!
* 132-CHARACTER LINE!
* UPPER AND LOWER CASE!
* STANDARD INTERFACE (RS-232 serial ASCII)!
* PIN-FEED OPTION AVAILABLE!
* TABING AND BACKSPACE UNDER COMPUTER CONTROL!
* LIMITED 30-DAY WARRANTY!
* ONLY $1,200!

Order C.O.D. from the Center for the Study of the Future, 4110 N. E. Alameda, Portland, OR 97212, (503) 282-5835.

TABLE 10-4: DESIGNING THE BROCHURE

1. Attract the reader's attention by identifying a need.
2. Relate your product to the need (see Table 10-5).
3. Do not promise what you cannot deliver.
4. Include all specifications, warranty information, and price.
5. Include purchasing methods (net 30 days, prepaid, C.O.D., VISA, or whatever).
6. Include an order form.
7. Study your competitors' brochures.
8. Design your brochure to fit in a standard envelope so that you can also use it with letters.
9. Key your brochure to its subject entry for filing purposes. For example, if the brochure describes a word processing system you might add: "Keyword Entry: word processing." The customer will then instantly know how to file your brochure, and it will more likely get filed, and filed quicker. Proper filing will mean better access should the need arise.

Shop around for your printer and get quotations before committing yourself, as prices can vary considerably. If possible, use a local printer. This is helpful (particularly if you are new at this) if the printer has questions or problems.

If you know a good wholesaler, buy the paper yourself. In some cases, a printer may purchase his paper in large sheets and cut it himself to save money. You might save by buying precut paper, but you may not. We like to use bright colors and high-quality paper. By selecting this ourselves, we know the printer will not cut corners. Specify to the printer the dimensions of the final copy, the kind of paper to use (if he buys it), the ink color, the number of copies to print, and any folding, binding, perforating, or collating necessary—all of which influence your cost. (The printer can easily enlarge or reduce your final copy to any necessary size.)

10.8 DIRECT MAIL SALES

Direct mail is an excellent sales approach for a small business with limited capital. You will need only to print brochures or letters, purchase a mailing list (preferably on peel-off labels), and start mailing information. Lead time to sales is short, so you will have a quick return on your investment.

Unlike display advertising, direct mail is person-to-person communication. It provides unlimited opportunity to tell a story intimately and directly. People like to get mail. Occasionally, complaints notwithstanding, motivational research experts have shown that direct mail advertising is welcomed. But people are bombarded with advertising material in magazines, radio, television and their mail. To compete and be heard, your message must strike a nerve. It must talk in the language of the reader and offer a benefit in which the reader is interested. When a letter spells out these benefits, the reader will read it and act on it.

There are many benefits that turn names on lists into buyers. These benefits can be categorized as follows:

time	prestige
money	skill
power	information
wealth	knowledge
security	happiness
attractiveness	love

For a businessman, these benefits can be interpreted as:

improved efficiency	increased sales
increased profits	reduced wastes
expanded markets	educated personnel
boosted output	enhanced morale
reduced costs	

Offer these benefits in your sales material and you'll sell.

Obtaining the appropriate mailing list can be as important as writing the right copy. Mailing lists vary in quality, so you have to be careful. Be sure the list you order is designed specifically for the market you want to reach. You can purchase mailing lists from many of the magazines in the appendix. You might also write to:

Resources	The Computer Faire
Box 134	Box 1579
Harvard Square	Palo Alto, CA 94302
Cambridge, MA 02138	($40/1000)
($70/3000–personal computing)	

You should try any computer show or computer-oriented magazine as well. In addition, you should obtain a copy of the most recent edition of *Direct Mail Lists Rates and Data*, a publication of Standard Rate and Data Service, Inc., 5201 Orchard Road, Skokie, IL 60076. This book is broken down into a variety of classifications targeted at specific audiences. For instance, you can buy a mailing list of all the businesses in your geographic area that have sales of $1,000,000 or less.

Check with your post office for information on mailing permits when you bulk mail your brochures.

If you are selling systems or a product at a fairly high cost, include a letter with the brochure and avoid the peel-off labels. Use your computer as a word processor and personalize the letter, being selective in your mailings.

Use your computer to keep track of your mailing response. A low-cost program for processing address labels is available from the Center for the Study of the Future (4110 N. E. Alameda, Portland, OR 97212) for $75. This is useful as you improve and add features onto your product. If people are happy with the product, they will want more.

10.9 MAGAZINE ADVERTISING

Be cautious with your advertising until you learn what sells. Experiment with low-cost ads unless you have had some experience with the market. Study your competitors'-ads. A big ad in a major magazine after the product has been out a while must mean this ad is working, even if the product is bad! If you use a small classified ad, make it short. Catch the readers' attention, inviting their response for your brochure. Avoid selling the product with the classfied ad; use short ads and a lot of repetition.

The *On-Line* magazine is a good place for initial ad purchases. The cost is low ($60 will get you several months' advertising), and you have a good monitor of whether your ad is working. In addition, this newsletter can get your ad to the reader in less than three weeks.

Once you find what sells, begin to purchase space in the larger magazines, keeping in mind the two-to-three-month lead time required for most magazines.

Cut out the better ads in magazines and post them in your work area. What makes the ad work? To what need of the reader does the ad relate?

10.10 LOCAL ADVERTISING

Your best approach here would be to use stores where possible customers will be purchasing. A friend of ours who sells used Selectric terminals leaves a stack of his business cards on the counters of electronic wholesalers and computer stores. He has a catchy business name, and his bright cards are easy to spot on the counters. Some stores have bulletin boards. Talk to your local computer stores and see if they are willing to sell your hardware or software on consignment. The store gets their percentage (about 30 percent on hardware, 40 percent on self-published books), and you get the remainder. With hardware and software this gives you an opportunity to test-market your product on a local level. You will get direct feedback from your customers, which will help greatly in improving your product. As the sales begin to grow, broaden your market beyond the local base.

Do not overlook local trade shows. In Portland, the word-processing suppliers get together once a year for a show at the Coliseum.

Publicity stunts are another good possibility. These could include: a temporary computer demonstration at the local science museum, free give-aways (frisbees, pencils, jumping coins and such), or writing a free-lance newspaper article on an unusual project.

Ads in local newspapers sometimes work; we have had both good and bad reports on this. If you buy a display ad, plan for a height of at least two inches in the business section. If you plan to use a classified advertisement, place it under business machines or office equipment categories. Some cities have special magazines with advertising only, but these seldom are read by the busy businessman. Use small ads and repeat them often.

10.11 ATTENDANCE AT FAIRS

Dozens of computer fairs are now being held each year, and establishing a booth at one of these is a very good method of introducing your product and getting direct customer feedback. Choose your fair carefully. What promotion of the fair will there be? Be specific in asking this question to the fair promoters and ask for proof. Even if you lose money at the fair, you will find that the questions prospective customers will ask will tell you specifically what the market needs are and how to develop a more comprehensive marketing program. We have found that the booth is hard work, but we have recovered at least enough money to pay for the trip. The educational value could not be measured in any amount of money. Small booths at the personal computing faires often sell for as little as $150. If money is limited, share a booth with someone else who is short on capital. Another idea is to target your showings to local fair where customers without computers will be attending; those who have already purchased computers go to larger computer fairs. Why not try advertising at a local boat show, home show, or camera show? These are held in every major city and will give you a good local exposure.

Your booth will be competing with many others for the customers' attention. In visiting fairs, walk around and study which exhibits catch your eye. Why? Model you exhibit after these. Try to touch the customer at as many senses as possible—sight, sound, smell, and taste. Use bright colors and use techniques to give the illusion of motion (as in printing Selectrics to sell printers, robots, or multimedia shows). Involve the participant in your display (as with games).

Bring your own table, satin drape and sign to the fair if you can. Make the sign so that it will fold up in a suitcase. Avoid any chairs in your booth—a busy salesman will never sit down. Establish eye contact with each customer and establish their need as early in the conversation as possible. A rug will make the job easier on your feet if the floor is concrete.

Assume that your equipment will not work when it is turned on. Get to your booth early and test everything, bringing back-up equipment if possible. Avoid changing the system at the last minute. Bring chart paper and a felt pen for dialogue purposes. You may also want to plan to give a speech around your skills and the product as a part of the program.

10.12 FOREIGN DISTRIBUTORSHIPS

You may feel, as a small garage-shop businessman, that you need not concern yourself with foreign sales. If you send a news release to the more popular computer magazines, however, you will find yourself getting numerous queries from foreign stores, distributors, and users, so you will need to establish some type of policy for foreign customers.

The level of involvement here includes a wide range of possibilities. We do, however, urge one word of caution. Employ legal help if you plan to establish any foreign distributorships; international protection of your hardware or software is complex.

11 HOW TO MAKE MONEY TEACHING OTHERS ABOUT COMPUTERS

A recent AFIPS study of the data processing industry predicts that by 1990 the total number of people working with computers will nearly double. It also predicts that computers will account for 13 percent of the total GNP.

The number of computer professionals today, and the number entering each year, won't be nearly enough to fill the vacancies. What this means is that there is going to be a tremendous need for education in the computer field. But where are the instructors going to come from?

If you can speak well on a general topic, you can help fill this void. Here are some courses you could teach to businessmen and/or small computer enthusiasts:

1. How to Use a Computer in Your Business
2. How to Program a Computer in BASIC (or other languages)
3. How a Computer Works

Like everything else, there are two ways to do it: teach the course for someone else, or handle it yourself. Let's start by examining the ways you can teach the course for someone else. The most common places to teach are in a high school or community college, a computer store, a computer center, or through a short course company.

11.1 THE COMMUNITY COLLEGE OR HIGH SCHOOL

If you would like to teach the fundamentals of microcomputers and learn a lot yourself, this is an excellent way to go. There are, however, two problems. First, the pay is terrible! Second, the institution may require you to have more education than is really necessary.

Many colleges have courses oriented to the microcomputer but don't have the necessary equipment. If you have your own equipment, you could plan an excellent "hands-on"-type course. The experience is good if you plan to build from this.

11.2 LOCAL COMPUTER STORE

Stores enjoy having classes for customers and potential customers. The constant visibility of the products during the classes enhance sales. Classes can be held in the evening after normal store hours so students can have an opportunity to tour the store and see the systems. Generally, plenty of demonstration systems are available and students can be exposed to a wide variety of software and hardware.

Pay is usually low, but teaching courses will give you an opportunity to work with a variety of systems. In addition, the class will give you credibility as a consultant.

11.3 COMPUTER CENTERS

The first computer center was founded in 1972 by Bob Albrecht. It originally operated out of a storefront in Menlo Park, California. You are probably familiar with at least its newsletter. We are, of course, referring to People's Computer Company.

The computing world has changed dramatically since then but the basic concept is still sound: *provide a place where people can come in off the street to learn about computers.*

If you don't have a computer center in your area you might consider opening one. Computer centers normally have plenty of low-cost systems that are cassette based. Students come in after school and write their own programs, paying a nominal charge for the computer time. Yearly memberships are also available, and classes are offered in a variety of computer-related topics. Again, the pay is low but the experience is worth it.

11.4 SHORT COURSE COMPANY

Short course companies offer the best opportunity for making money. You are probably already familiar with some of these companies, such as Osborne, Sybex, Wintek, and ICS. All pay extremely well, but opportunities are limited. Most people that teach for these companies have a Ph.D. and a few years' teaching experience. You can, however, teach for manufacturers, computer shows and the like with less education and less experience. The best way to find out about this is to contact some manufacturers in your area.

11.5 HOLDING YOUR OWN SHORT COURSE

If you are an established teacher, author, or consultant, you can offer workshops and lectures at hotels or motels that have conference facilities. Even without the organizational support of a short course company, you can have a successful program if you can market yourself and the course.

Pay is good ($200 or more per student), but student expectations are high. This type of program requires newspaper advertising, a well-defined course outline, plenty of audio-visual materials and handouts, and course material targeted specifically for a broad base of needs.

Notice also that the federal government has recently taken an interest in "vocational schools," restricting their activities in important ways. The promises you make or imply in your promotion structure, or course material will be noted by those who disapprove of you. As ever, don't fail to deliver at least what you promise, even inadvertantly.

11.6 MAIL ORDER COURSE

The mail order course offers the advantage that it need not appeal to a broad-based market. Specialty subjects such as microcomputer circuit design, advanced programming, and software graphics techniques can easily be addressed. Courses can include books, audio cassettes, programming cassettes, floppy disc software, and/or video cassettes.

Your profit is limited only by your marketing skill. Courses can be sold to individuals, businesses and schools. In some cases you may need to include hardware. (Speechlab is a good example of a mail order course that includes hardware.)

A mail order course can also be designed as a self-study course. In self-study courses, the student is guided through the material at his own pace. This can be done with specific textbook design or with a computer program, using a good high-level language like PILOT.

Developing a mail order course is a time-consuming job that takes a tremendous amount of work, dedication and patience. The rewards are certainly worth it, but it is not something you should go into until you have a considerable amount of teaching experience.

11.7 PREPARING THE COURSE

The first step in preparing any course is defining the specific learning goals. When your student has completed the course, what specific knowledge or capability should he/she have? What knowledge or capability should the student bring to the class? Answer these questions in writing and carefully analyze your answers.

How can you best serve your students? The purpose of this is to ensure that you will include all important material without loading the student with material that he/she will not need.

Now you can establish the course outline based on your input (what the student brings to the class) and your output (what the student learns from the class). (As there are several similarities in writing a course and writing a book, you should review Chapter 2 before you prepare your course.) You can get a good grasp on what you hope to accomplish in the course by deciding how you are going to evaluate the students. Spot quizzes, for instance, can help you evaluate student progress at key points.

Courses sell systems and your skill as a consultant. It is easy to impress students, but you must keep in mind that your primary purpose is to share knowledge. You can best do this by keeping the class goal in mind at all times.

11.8 POSSIBLE COURSE OUTLINES

In this section, we will review some possible course outlines. These are intended only as examples of what you can do.

Course A: How to Use a Computer in Your Business

    I.   Do you really need a computer in your business?
        A. What the computer can and cannot do for you.
        B. How large a business do you have?

II. How to Select a Computer
    A. What are your needs?
    B. Differences between minicomputers and micro-computers
       1. Capabilities
       2. Cost
III. How a Computer Works
IV. What is Computer Software?
    A. Kinds of software
    B. Where to find it
V. What Kinds of Warranties are Available?
VI. What Kind of Maintenance is Available?

Course B: How to Program a Computer in BASIC

I. Introduction to BASIC Programming
    A. The digital computer
    B. BASIC
    C. Simple complete BASIC programs
    D. Running BASIC programs on a timeshared computer
    E. Running BASIC programs using batch processing
II. Arithmetic Operations
    A. Addition, subtraction, multiplication and division
    B. Exponentiation
    C. Hierarchy of arithmetic operations
    D. Use of parentheses
    E. Assigning values—LET and equals sign
    F. Precision—accuracy—overflow and underflow
III. Input and Output Statements
    A. The READ and DATA statements
    B. The RESTORE statement
    C. The INPUT statement
    D. The PRINT statement
    E. Printing of text—use and input and output
    F. The PRINTUSING statement
    G. The TAB specifier
    H. The SETDIGITS statement
IV. Control Statements
    A. The GO TO statement
    B. The IF-THEN statement
    C. The STOP statement
    D. Flow charts
    E. Documentation

II. Number Systems
   A. The basic ideas of number systems
   B. Changing from one base to another
   C. Some elementary binary arithmetic
III. Basic Computer Elements
   A. Logical notation
   B. Gates
   C. Interconnection of gates to obtain other gates
   D. The adder
   E. The multiplexer
   F. Flip-flops
   G. Clocking
   H. Registers
   I. Counters
   J. Sequence detectors and sequence generators
IV. Memories
   A. Semiconductor memories
   B. Paralleling of memory devices
   C. Magnetic RAMs
   D. Read only memories—ROMs
   E. Tape, disc and drum memories
   F. Codes
V. Basic Digital Computation
   A. The basic arithmetic logic unit
   B. Modular arithmetic
   C. 2's complement arithmetic
   D. Multiplication and division
   E. Floating point numbers
VI. The Digital Computer
   A. The general organization of a digital computer
   B. Memory commands—information transmission
   C. Entering and execution of instructions
   D. The complete digital computer
   E. Machine language programming
   F. Assembler language
   G. Loaders
   H. Higher level languages
VII. Computer Applications
   A. Comparison of computers
   B. Things that can be done with a computer

VIII.   Available Small Computers
        A. Microprocessors
        B. Complete small computers
        C. Peripherals

12 HOW TO ESTABLISH A BUSINESS

If you plan on using your computer to create income, you should plan to establish your enterprise as a business to identify it legally, to track accounting, and to improve cash flow. Your business can be established as a sole proprietorship, a partnership, or a corporation. Each of these has advantages and disadvantages, so it is important to get enough legal information before you start your business to give yourself maximum advantage in reaching your desired goals. It is a wise idea to get legal help, so if you don't have capital available to spend on legal advice, find a friend who has established a similar type of business and talk over your plans with him. Visit your local Small Business Administration office. The federal government has many free and very helpful materials for the small businessman.

12.1 SOLE PROPRIETORSHIP

When is a hobby a business? You can establish your system as a business entity if you can show a profit two out of every five years. This income is reported on Schedule C with your income tax and is taxed as ordinary income. In addition, you must deduct a 7.9 percent social security tax using Schedule SE. This is the simplest way to set up any business and avoids the legal hassles of a partnership or a corporation. The business is owned by you and is classed legally as a sole proprietorship. In some municipalities, any business operated out of a home must be registered with the city. In Portland, for example, a homeowner must have the signatures of 66 percent of his near neighbors on a petition to operate a business out of his home, and there are many restrictions on a residential business (no signs, no customers or unusual traffic, etc.). This may sound like a lot of work, but it can give you a good opportunity to meet your neighbors and perhaps establish a few business contacts. We found that when neighbors listened to our story and understood the city-controlled restrictions, there was little problem in their signing our petition.

You will also need to check with your county, and if you have a business name, register it with the state. Choice of a name is an important decision! It should be catchy so as to draw interest, it should communicate the type of business you have, and it should be short.

With some professions, special licenses also may be necessary in some states. If you have any employees, you will need to check for tax regulations at federal, state, county, and municipal levels.

Your accounting system can either be set up on a cash basis or on the accrual basis. With an accounting system on the cash basis, you report income in the taxable year you receive it and deduct expenses in the taxable year paid. If your accounting system is on the accrual basis, you report income that has been earned, whether received or not, and deduct expenses incurred, whether paid or not. The IRS does not care which system you use as long as you are consistent. Any amounts credited to your account and under your control, however, must be done on a cash basis. The cash basis has a distinct advantage for most small businesses: With your business on a cash basis, you have more control of cash flow. You should use your computer to handle your accounting. As you near the end of your business year, you should be able to "project" your spending with your accounting program and plan your cash flow in the last month to minimize taxes. After the first year, you should be able to project cash flow for succeeding years.

When your start, you can probably base your business from your home. There are several advantages to this: very few home businesses fail; expenses are low, and you can do everything yourself. This means overhead is low, so you should be able to keep your prices below competition. Travel time is zero, since you do not have to drive to or from an office, giving you a few more productive hours in the day. You should be happier, have less tensions, be healthier, and live longer as your own boss.

There are some situations in which you should *not* use your home. The home business should not be detrimental to family life; your family is more important than the business. How well behaved are the kids? Do they leave your desk and work areas alone? Are they noisy? Are you productive in the home environment? These issues must be weighed against the advantages of the home business.

If you operate your computer as a business, the IRS allows you to deduct all relevant expenses, such as the computer itself, other peripherals, your telephone, trade journal subscriptions, mileage and car travel, computer show trips, stationery, and other office supplies. To permit deducting part of your residence as an expense, you can only deduct that portion of your residence that is used regularly and exclusively as a principal place of business. If your office qualifies, you can deduct the fair market rental value of the space and relevant electricity, gas, repairs, etc.

The actual expenditure for your computer is a capital expense and is *not* deductible. The IRS does, however, permit you to deduct the depreciation of the computer over the year. The easiest method would be to assume that your equipment has a seven-year life and deduct on a straight line depreciation. If you purchased a system valued at $7,500, with a value of $500 after seven years, the depreciation allowed on your taxes would be $1,000 a year!

$$
\begin{array}{ll}
\$7,500 & \text{system cost} \\
\underline{500} & \text{salvage value after seven years} \\
\$7,000 &
\end{array}
$$

Depreciation/year $(7,000/7) = \$1,000$

In addition, the IRS allows you an investment credit of 10 percent in the year in which the equipment is purchased. This is subtracted from your taxes after calculation. For a $7,500 system, this means you would pay $750 less in taxes the first year. To claim the 10 percent investment credit, the equipment must have a useful life of seven years or more. (This is quite reasonable for microcomputers.) Remember, this investment credit is allowable only during the first year when the equipment is purchased and is subtracted from your taxes after the tax calculation. The investment credit requires a separate IRS form.

Check on two other IRS forms: forms 5212 and 5214. In many cases you will need to submit these. Another idea is to disallow some of your expenses in the early years to permit your business to show a profit in two out of the five years required. Check the references in Appendix F for more details.

Software is considered an expense unless purchased as part of a hardware system. As such, it is 100 percent deductible in the year it is purchased and is not allowable for investment credit.

As a sole proprietorship, you are 100 percent liable for the debts of the business. If you become liable for damages, any or all of your personal assets can be legally claimed in a lawsuit—the primary disadvantage of the sole proprietorship. The advantage is that it is far easier to administrate than is a corporation or partnership. You will spend less time with red tape and have more free time for the creative aspects of your business.

12.2 PARTNERSHIPS

Partnerships are similar to sole proprietorships, with each partner reporting his share of the income. No "wages" are reported—all is income. In addition, form 1065 is filed.

One advantage of the partnership is that capital gains, income, depreciation methods, and such can be proportioned out to the tax advantage of each.

The family offers an ideal partnership opportunity, as the income from a family member in a high tax bracket can be shifted to one in a lower tax bracket.

Be careful to put your partnership agreement on paper and get legal advice on its establishment. There are two types: a general partnership and a limited partnership. With a general partnership, each partner is liable for obligations incurred by the business; no state permission is required. In a limited partnership, each agrees to a percentage of the profits, but the liabilities are not assumed on the same percentage. An example of this would be a partner who loans you money to start the business but does not wish to assume the liabilities. A limited partnership must be registered with the state.

12.3 CORPORATION

A corporation is the most complex form of business organization. It is a separate legal "being," born the moment it is created. It can be sued, enter into contracts, and pay taxes just as an individual.

The corporation is a state-defined entity. To form a corporation, you register with the state, not the federal government. Laws and costs vary from state to state, so in some states (as Delaware) it is relatively easy to form a corporation; even someone living elsewhere can form a corporation, registering it in Delaware. In other states it is considerably more difficult and time consuming.

The corporation defines its own tax year and files its own tax return (Form 1120) with the federal government just as an individual taxpayer does. The tax year should be chosen so that the books do not close in the middle of your busiest season; and' it does not have to coincide with the day the corporation was formed. As a result, your first federal return may represent a short year.

Corporations can be organized for a variety of purposes. Some are organized on a nonprofit basis for educational, charitable, or religious purposes. Others are organized to make a profit. In the past, many corporations have filed with the IRS as nonprofit to gain tax advantages or to qualify for grants. This process subsequently has been abused and, as a result, the IRS now has made the process very difficult. If you plan for all the profits of the corporation to be your personal income, the income is reported as an expense for the corporation and as income on your personal 1040 form (this income has to be reasonable, however). The corporation profit is zero, as there would be no profit to tax. The primary advantage of this nonprofit status would be in minimizing property taxes or if you need to qualify for a grant. In this case you would be wise to seek legal help.

12.4 THE DECISION TO INCORPORATE

When should incorporation be considered a usable option for your business? To make this decision, you should study both the advantages and disadvantages (Table 12-1). When the advantages outweigh the disadvantages, you should begin to pursue incorporation.

The corporation is a separate legal entity. If someone sues the corporation and the corporation does not have enough assets, the court cannot hold you personally liable for the debts of the

TABLE 12-1: PROS AND CONS OF INCORPORATING

PROS	*CONS*
You gain legal protection. You, as an individual, cannot be held legally liable for the debts of the corporation.	Social security tax will be higher—11.7 percent versus 7.9 percent as a sole proprietor.
You can establish tax-sheltered pension, life insurance, hospital insurance, and bonus plans at the cost of the corporation.	You will have to pay an unemployment tax to the state.
Your income from the corporation becomes an expense.	More time involved with extra paper work and meetings.
The survival of the corporation is independent of the owners. The corporation can survive after your death if you establish it properly.	License expenses will involve extra paper work and meetings. Corporate income is taxed at 20 percent of the first $25,000.
Corporate shares are assets and can be sold or purchased. As such, the sale of stock can be used to raise venture capital.	
Incorporating gives you business privacy.	

corporation. The only exception to this is if you organize a corporation purposely to defraud. The corporation is owned by the stockholders, and the operating decisions of the corporation are made by a board of directors elected by the stockholders. Those who work for the corporation are employees of the corporation, and the same people may be employees, stockholders, and member of the board of directors. In most states, only one to three people are required to form a corporation, and they all may be from your immediate family.

Incorporating gives you a business name. Your business can gain venture capital and business loans easier because it is incorporated. You can also establish a wide range of fringe benefits as expenses to the corporation, which are tax free. These include tax-sheltered pensions, life insurance, hospital and health insurance, and accident insurance. As a sole proprietorship, you would have to pay taxes on your income for these expenses. As a corporation, these are tax free.

Incorporating also has its disadvantages. You will have two tax returns to complete each year: your personal form and that of the corporation. The corporation tax form probably will require help from a tax specialist. Often you will have special forms for the state, county, and city as well as the federal return. A corporation also takes considerable time to organize and operate.

You may not necessarily save money by incorporating. A corporation is taxed at 20 percent of its first $25,000. If the corporate assets in cash or negotiables is more than $150,000, you must declare a dividend unless you have definite capital expansion plans for these assets (such as the purchase of property) and can document these plans for the IRS.

12.5 THE PROCESS OF INCORPORATING

The easiest and best way to incorporate is to find a competent lawyer and let him handle the process. Although this is the most expensive alternative, we strongly recommend it. A lawyer can show you ways of organizing your corporation to minimize taxes and give you maximum profit, and you will probably be able to recover the lawyer's fee in operating expenses the first year. Do not underestimate the expert advice of legal help. Your legal fees may vary from about $100 to $800 for incorporating, but do not shop for low cost—shop for competency and someone you can trust. Preferably, you should find a lawyer who specializes in setting up corporations.

The name of your corporation is the next important decision. This name must be unique in your state. Most companies go to considerable expense to build a reputation on their names. The state protects this name, prohibiting anyone else from using it. You have to create a unique name and build your own reputation, the name should be short and communicate something about the type of business in which the corporation is involved.

This name should be filed with the state and registered as early as possible. Often, it is wise to send a second or third choice in case your first choice is not available. Some cost is involved in registering this name, and the registration fee will have to paid annually to protect your name.

Stock can be either common (one vote per share and rights to dividends) or preferred (special dividends paid before other dividends but generally no vote). Most companies incorporate with about 200 shares of common stock.

12.6 INCORPORATING AS A SUBCHAPTER S CORPORATION

To make your tax return as simple as possible, you can elect to be a Subchapter S Corporation. This enables you to report the corporation income on Form C of your income tax, just as if you were a sole proprietorship, rather than as an expense to the corporation. This offers all the advantages of the corporation in terms of limited personal liability, yet gives you advantages of the simplified tax reporting of the sole proprietorship. To qualify as a Subchapter S Corporation:

1. All stockholders must be individuals.
2. There can be no more than ten stockholders.
3. Your business must be a domestic corporation.
4. There can only be one class of stock.
5. Over 80 percent of the gross receipts must come from income other than royalties, rents, dividends, interest, annuities, gains on sales, exchanges of stock, or securities.

13 HOW TO MANAGE YOUR BUSINESS

Management is the science of controlling resources to obtain a desired goal. The manager has certain resources, such as money, people and equipment, that are input to the system. How you will manage the resources will determine how successful you are.

Whether you manage a large group of people or just yourself, there are some basic principles you should follow. Basically, the manager does only five things:

1. *Sets Objectives.* You determine what the objectives should be and the goal of each objective. Once you have determined these two things, you decide what has to be done to realize these objectives. Lastly, you make the objectives effective by carefully directing the activities of the people who carry out the objectives.

2. *Organizes.* You analyze all activities, decisions and relationships within your business. You then classify all work and divide it into manageable activities. Next, group these activities into an organizational structure, determining who does what, and assign priorities.

3. *Motivates and Communicates.* You make a team out of the people who work for you. If you have a lot of employees, you will have several sub-teams, all working as cohesive units. The primary thing you must remember and instill in your employees is: *the good of the company is always more important that any personality*. Do not let anyone's personal problem or quirk interfere with the smooth operation of your business.

4. *Measures.* You must constantly monitor your employees. This means you analyze, appraise and interpret their performance. How are they doing? Can anyone do a better job? Is someone performing better than could be expected? Why?
5. *Develops People, Including Himself.* Real genius in management is the ability to take someone who has no background and little or no aptitude for a particular task and develop a first-rate performer. Everyone has something they are really good at. Find it and develop it.

13.1 CHANGING PARADIGMS

Most managers subscribe to an industrial-age paradigm that defines work as "picking up a burden reluctantly because we are forced to do so by some external morality." If we are not being productive, we feel or experience guilt. This paradigm is programmed into most of us by our cultural forces. If we wish to really discover excitement and meaning in life, we have to break free of these pressures.

Abraham Maslow defined a new concept of management in his book, *Eupsychian Management* (Homewood, Illinois: Richard D. Irwin, Inc., 1965), in which the goal becomes that of releasing people to their full creativity. These concepts developed by Maslow hold only under good market conditions and will not work when the primary need drives are security and survival. The exciting premise, however, is that those of us working in the microcomputer business are experiencing unprecedented growth, success and acceptance. Companies and organizations working at this frontier should be able to implement Maslow's theories. What, then, are the basics of his concepts?

Maslow defined about three dozen basic concepts which could be summarized as:

1. Assume everyone can be trusted. (If he cannot be trusted, why is he accepted—or hired—as a part of your program?)
2. Assume everyone wants to achieve and be successful.
3. Be open with information and facts. Keep everyone informed!
4. The order is older-brotherly rather than authoritarian.
5. Assume synergy and good will.
6. Assume the organization and individuals are healthy.
7. Affirm and celebrate successes.

8. All basic needs, such as survival, security and safety, must be already met.
9. There should be good teamwork, brotherhood, love and group harmony.
10. All work should be meaningful.
11. Call out the uniqueness of the individuals.
12. Make veryone feel important for what they can give to the project as an individual.

Today's most successful managers define goals in terms of these principles. They learn to think in a different way about how to organize to reach these goals and implement the feedback necessary to insure that these goals are met. The ball game is entirely different.

People cannot be treated as capital, money or equipment. The only thing your company has that no other company has is the creativity and uniqueness of those who work with you. Encourage this. Helping your employees with their education and with trips to conferences will encourage them and motivate their creativity. If you do not do this as a manager, you will find that your people will still take additional courses and go to conferences, but the knowledge they gain will be channeled to personal goals and projects. These projects will be quite successful in the age of the microcomputer revolution, and you will lose a good employee.

If you keep these as organizational principles, you should not be too surprised to find people volunteering to work with you on your projects. As long as their basic needs are met, people seek self-actualization. When a project sounds exciting and along the lines of their own personal goals, they will join communities (organizations) that are moving toward these goals. In any case, you should allow time in your project for sharing and relating at a personal level. Learn to see employees as creative people, not as depersonalized resources.

13.2 USING YOUR COMPUTER AS PART OF THE MANAGEMENT PROCESS

Your computer can be a tool in your organization. It should be capable of routine management work, leaving you free for the more creative aspects of management. You will need good software for project control of both time and cost. As goals and schedules change with time, the computer can be a great asset, helping you reschedule activities and costs as factors change.

13.3 A PROJECT MANAGEMENT PROGRAM

As an example of how a computer can be used to control project flow, we developed a very simple program in BASIC to write task schedules, and arrange and sort them on a priority basis. The program is shown in Figure 13.1. It is written in Commercial BASIC but can be altered easily for other BASICs. It is based on time management methods described by Alan Lakein in *How to Get Control of Your Time and Your Life* (Peter H. Wyden, Inc., 1973).

To create the initial task file, list all your current projects on a sheet of paper, and the dates for which each needs to be completed. Then prioritize each task, with "A" representing the most important, "B" the next most important, and "C" for the next. Alter the programs so that the task file has either your name or an input statement that asks the name of the task file. When the program is started, answer the first question with a "y" to create this file. The program will then ask for an operation mode:

u—update the current file or create a new file.
l—sort and list the current file
p—sort and print (on the printer) the current file
e—exit

The "l" and "p" modes both use the same routine, with the only difference being the output device. The "e" mode returns the user to the operating system (see Figure 13.1).

The update mode, when requested, asks the user for the type of update option required:

a—add an item
d—delete an item
p—alter priority on an item
e—exit update mode

The initial file is created with the "a" option. You can add as many tasks as you desire, and then use the "e" to return to the main program to print these with a "p" mode.

```
CBASIC COMPILER VER 1.00
 1:  Rem Personal Management Program
 2:  rem by Carl Townsend
 3:  rem last edit date: 1/15/78
 4:          carl.asc$="carl.asc"
 5:          print "Personal Management Program":print
 6:          true = -1
 7:          Input "Create a New File? ";i$
 8:          if left$(i$,1)="y" then goto 80
 9:          open carl.asc$ recl 80 as 1
10: 10       n=1
11:          if end # 1 then 90
12:          read # 1,1;q
13:          input "Option (update, list, print or exit): ";i$
14:          if left$(i$,1)="l" then goto 21
15:          if left$(i$,1)="p" then goto 20
16:          if left$(i$,1)="u" then goto 30
17:          if left$(i$,1)="e" then goto 90
18:          goto 10
19: 20 rem   print mode
20:          lprinter
21: 21 rem   list mode
22:          input "Date: ";d$
23:          print:print "Personal Task Schedule":print
24:          print "Date: ";d$
25:          print
26:          flag = true
27:          if end # 1 then 25
28:          while flag = true
29:              n=2
30:              flag = false
31:              read # 1,n;i$
32:              while q-n
33:                  read # 1,n+1;j$
34:                  if left$(i$,1)>left$(j$,1) then
35:                      k$=i$: i$=j$: j$=k$: flag = true
36:                  print # 1,n;i$
37:                  i$=j$
38:                  n=n+1
39:              wend
40:              print # 1,n ;j$
41:          wend
42: 25       n=2
43:          if end # 1 then 10
44: 27       read # 1,n;i$
```

```
45:           i$=" "+i$
46:           print using "##";n-1;: print i$
47:           n=n+1
48:           if (n-1)<>q then goto 27
49:           console
50:           goto 10
51: 30 rem    update mode
52:           read # 1,1;q
53:           input "Priority alter, delete,add or exit: ";i$
54:           if left$(i$,1) ="p" then goto 40
55:           if left$(i$,1) ="d" then goto 50
56:           if left$(i$,1) ="a" then goto 60
57:           if left$(i$,1) ="e" then goto 10
58:           goto 30
59: 40 rem    priority alter option
60:           input "Item # :";n
61:           if n > (q-1) then goto 30
62:           read # 1,n+1;i$
63:           print "Job: ";i$
64:           input "New Priority: ";p$
65:           i$=left$(p$,1)+mid$(i$,2,len(i$)-1)
66:           print # 1,n+1;i$
67:           goto 30
68: 50 rem    delete option
69:           input "Item # :";n
70:           if n > (q-1) then goto 30
71:           if n=q-1 then print # 1,1;q-1:goto 30
72:           for s=n+1 to q-1
73:           read # 1,n+2;i$
74:           print # 1,n+1;i$
75:           n=n+1
76:           next s
77:           read # 1,1;s
78:           print # 1,1,s-1
79:           goto 30
80: 60 rem    add option
81:           input "Job Description: ";j$
82:           input "Priority: ";p$
83:           input "Date: ";d$
84:           i$=left$(p$,1)+" "+left$(d$,8)+" "+j$
85:           q=q+1
86;           if len(i$) > 78 then i$=left$(i$,78)
87:           print q-1;" ";i$
88:           print # 1,q;i$
89:           print # 1,1;q
90:           goto 30
```

```
91: 80 rem   create new file
92:          create carl.asc$ recl 80 as 1
93:          n=1:print # 1,1;n
94:          goto 10
95: 90 rem   close files
96:          close 1
97:          stop
98:          end
NO ERRORS DETECTED
```

Figure 13.1. Personal Management Program

crun task

CRUN VER 1.01

Personal Management Program

Create a New File? n

Option (update, list, print or exit): p

Date: 01/16/78

Personal Task Schedule

Date: 01/16/78

1	A	01/14/78	Write letters (Center)
2	A	01/14/78	Next Patterns
3	A	01/18/78	Continue writing book
4	A	01/18/78	Document Personal Management Program
5	A	01/18/78	Mailout—Sort Module
6	A	01/25/78	Do coordinate maps
7	A	01/18/78	Repair tape recorder for church
8	A	01/21/78	Read Winter's book
9	A	02/15/78	Church Information System—proposal
10	B	01/25/78	Mailout—Update Module
11	B	01/25/78	Mailout—Extraction Module
12	B	01/31/78	Read—corporation books
13	B	01/31/78	Read—book on volunteer organizations
14	B	01/25/78	Business Proposal
15	B	02/15/78	Assemble 2SIO and Floppy Disk Interface
16	C	02/28/78	Income Tax—calculate
17	C	02/28/78	Nutrition Program
18	C	02/15/78	Checkout 2SIO and interface

Option (update, list, print or exit): e

Figure 13.2. Sample Project Listing

```
crun task
CRUN VER 1.01
Personal Management Program
Create a New File? n
Option (update, list, print or exit): u
Priority alter, delete, add or exit: a
Job Description: Accounting Program
Priority: B
Date: 01/31/78
19  B   01/31/78  Accounting Program
Priority alter, delete, add or exit: d
Item # : 12
Priority alter, delete, add or exit: p
Item # : 5
Job: A  01/18/78     Mailout—Sort Module
New Priority: B
Priority alter, delete, add or exit: e
Option (update, list, print or exit): l
Date:   01/17/78
Personal Task Schedule
Date:   01/17/78

  1  A  01/14/78   Write letters (Center)
  2  A  01/14/78   Next Patterns
  3  A  01/18/78   Continue writing book
  4  A  01/18/78   Document Personal Management Program
  5  A  01/25/78   Do coordinate maps
  6  A  01/18/78   Repair tape recorder for church
  7  A  01/21/78   Read Winter's book
  8  A  02/15/78   Church Information System—proposal
  9  B  01/18/78   Mailout—Sort Module
 10  B  01/25/78   Mailout—Update Module
 11  B  01/25/78   Mailout—Extraction Module
 12  B  01/31/78   Read—book on volunteer organizations
 13  B  01/25/78   Business Proposal
 14  B  02/15/78   Assemble 2SIO and Floppy Disk Interface
 15  B  01/31/78   Accounting Program
 16  C  02/28/78   Income Tax—calculate
 17  C  02/28/78   Nutrition Program
 18  C  02/15/78   Checkout 2SIO and interface
Option (update, list, print or exit): e
```

Figure 13.3 Sample of Update

There are many other ways to use your computer in your business. If you would like a specific example of how to use it, you will want to read *From the Counter to the Bottom Line*, by Carl Warren and Merl Miller (dilithium Press).

We hope this book will serve as a starting point for making money with your microcomputer. In the future, we would like to put together a book of money-making computer projects. If you have an idea, please write us in care of Robotics Press. We look forward to hearing from you. Happy computing!

A GRANTS AND PROPOSALS

Grants are obtained primarily from two sources: foundations and the government. Foundation grants are available only if your organization is classified by the IRS as a public foundation. Government grants are available to any individual or organization.

The major problem in getting grants is getting the first one. Your proposal will be in competition with experts who write proposals professionally to earn their living. Many of the professionals who write proposals have recognized names and can win proposals from being recognized as specialists in a particular discipline. It is very difficult for someone who has not worked to get money this way before to sell his (or her) first proposal.

A.1 GETTING FOUNDATION GRANTS

The best place to start for foundation grants is the local library or educational research center. Locate their foundation directories; local areas often publish directories of local foundations and their funding patterns over the last few years. These local directories are quite inexpensive ($8 for the Portland directory) and a must for someone starting in business. This type of directory will give information on the smaller foundations that are the best sources for your first grant.

Another important tool is the Lockheed Data Base in California (3251 Hanover Street, Palo Alto, CA 94304). Their Foundation Grants Index is a record of foundation funding by subject areas over the last few years. This can be accessed on a subscription basis from any terminal using the telephone line. Most major cities already have several terminals plugged into this system. In Portland, the Northwest Regional Educational Laboratory maintains a terminal to the Lockheed system.

If you have your own terminal and modem, you can subscribe to the service yourself. If this system is new to you, it is best to work with someone familiar with it in starting.

The cost for this foundation search is about $40 to $90 for most subject areas. This Lockheed system—better known as Dialog—can also search for information published on any subject. We recently ran a subject search on community networking using computers on the Dialog system and got 161 citations. This type of search is helpful to locate who is doing what. Your project should not duplicate what someone else is doing.

Individuals are rarely able to capture foundation grants, as IRS restrictions make it necessary for foundations to manage their funding carefully. To qualify for grants from a foundation, your organization must be classed as a public foundation under 501 (c) (3). You also must be organized and operated for public safety or a recognized church, school, hospital, governmental body or public charity. In addition, you must receive more than one-third of your support from the general public and not more than one-third from investments (bonds, stocks, etc.). If you qualify, you can submit Form 4653 to the IRS and receive your M 0712 form from them, indicating that you comply. A copy of this M 0712 form should be included with your proposal. This routine may sound simple, but in most cases you may require help from a lawyer. You will spend considerable time and do a lot of work.

The alternative would be to work through an existing organization that already qualifies. Your church or place of employment may fit into these categories, so you can write the proposal under their sponsorship. The organization can then contract the work to you as an individual or to your organization.

A.2 WINNING YOUR PROPOSAL FROM A FOUNDATION

Winning your proposal will be hard work. Your start should be a query letter and appointment with the executive director of the foundation. If you have influential contacts, you will find these extremely important. Identify the specific interests of the foundation and sponsoring organization, and write your proposal to approach these interests—*not* your own.

As you write the proposal, keep several points in mind:

1. Identify the need and why it is not being met by any current programs. Show the importance of the need being met.
2. Show how your project will meet this need.
3. Include organizational responsibility, PERT time charts, budget, and resumes of all pertinent leadership. Include your labor and the cost of any computer time on your own system.

Several ideas that are looking for proposals are shown in Table A-1. A sample proposal outline is shown in Table A-2.

TABLE A-1: PROPOSAL IDEAS

1. Using the microcomputer to help the handicapped.
2. Using microcomputer systems in community memory and information networking.
3. Using the microcomputer for computer conferencing and electronic mail.
4. Software development for using the computer in teaching (as the PILOT program).
5. Simulation programs for high schools and colleges (political decisions, land use decisions, energy resource allocation, financial management).

(The National Science Foundation and the Department of Health, Education and Welfare, as well as local special interest groups, are funding proposals in these areas.)

After submission of the proposal, be prepared to make a subsequent oral presentation as a follow-up. As a foundation board may meet only one to four times a year, you may have to wait several months—unless you know the exact time the board meets, and plan for this presentation date in submitting the proposal.

We highly advise anyone pursuing this route to check the publications in Table A-3, particularly Dermer's *How to Raise Funds From Foundations*. You can save money by checking with local organizations that do a lot of proposal writing and borrowing their copies of the better publications on writing

TABLE A-2: PROPOSAL OUTLINE

I.   Introduction

What is the specific need to which you plan to relate? Why is this need important?

II. Perspective

What is the historical perspective on the problem? How has the problem been resolved previously? How is the need being met now? Is this adequate? What new factors are acting to alter the previous ways in which this need was met? What surveys have you taken on this need and what were the results? What is the history of your work with the problem and what has it indicated?

III. Objective or Purpose

What specific way will you or your organization meet this need? How will you determine your success? What criteria will be used to measure it? Who will benefit (people, groups, organizations)? What is unique about your approach?

IV. Planning Overview

What are your plans for accomplishing your objectives? (Define in multi-phase steps using PERT or critical path charting.) Define long- and short-term objectives. What resources are necessary (people, finances, organizations)? Is your budget as tight as it could be?

V.   Project Management

What is unique about your skills or those of your organization; What is your "track record?" Who is involved? What are his or her qualifications for the job? To whom are you accountable? What is your financial status? Legal status?

VI. Future Plans

What could evolve from the project? How does it relate to other needs? What are some future possibilities?

VII. Conclusion

proposals. You also might have some of them check the early drafts of your proposal for suggestions and criticisms. Find some sample proposals that were successful and study these.

The route may seem long and difficult, but the long-term rewards can be great. If your first proposal is a winner and you complete it on schedule with the anticipated results, you will find that putting the next proposal together is less work, and more of your time can be put into development. Using your computer as a word processor, you can store proposal parts and paragraphs on your system and create new proposals in very little time.

TABLE A-3: RESOURCES FOR FOUNDATION GRANTS

Dermer, Joseph, *How to Raise Funds From Foundations*, Public Service Materials Center, 355 Lexington Ave., New York, NY

How to Write Successful Foundation Presentations, Public Service Materials Center, 1975.

Proposal Guidelines, Educational Innovators Press, P. O. Box 13052, Tucson, AZ 85711, 1971.

A.3 GETTING GOVERNMENT GRANTS

The place to start for getting government money is the *Catalogue of Federal Domestic Assistance*, available at your local library. Use this to identify the programs in which you are interested. Now ask the library for the *Federal Register*. This will give you more information on the program as to the rules and regulations, application deadlines, priorities and funding cycles. You may find the *Register* difficult to use, but learning to use it will teach you some of the vocabulary and procedures you will need to win your grant. The third step is to call the government agency and ask to speak with whoever is in charge of the project. Get the application package and as much additional information as possible.

As with a foundation proposal, create your outline (as in A.2) and build your proposal around this outline. You should also look at the sample business plan in the marketing chapter for additional ideas on the proposal outline.

B COMPUTER MAGAZINES

BYTE Magazine
70 Main Street
Peterborough, NH 03458

Computer
IEEE
5855 Naples Plaza
Suite 301
Long Beach, CA 90803

Computer Data
Whitsed Pub., Ltd.
Suite 2504
2 Bloor Street West
Toronto, CANADA M4W 3GI

Computer Dealer Magazine
Gordon Publications
P. O. Box 2106-M
Morristown, NJ 07960

Computer Design
11 Goldsworth Ave.
Littleton, MA 01460

Computer Music Journal
Box E
Menlo Park, CA 94025

Computer Product News
CEMCON
4 North Elmhurst Rd.
Prospect Heights, IL 60070

Computer Retailing
1760 Peachtree Rd., NW
Atlanta, GA 30357

ComputerWorld
797 Washington Street
Newton, MA 02160

Creative Computing
Box 789M
Morristown, NJ 07960

Data Communications
McGraw Hill Publications
645 N. Michigan Ave.
Chicago, IL 60611

Datamation
1801 S. La Cienega Blvd.
Los Angeles, CA 90035

Digital Design
Benwill Publishing Co.
1050 Commonwealth Ave.
Boston, MA 02215

Dr. Dobb's Journal of
   Computer Calisthenics &
   Orthodontia
Box E
Menlo Park, CA 94025

EDN
221 Columbus Ave.
Boston, MA 02116

Electronic Design
50 Essex Street
Rochelle Part, NJ 07662

Electronic Engineering Times
280 Community Drive
Great Neck, NY 11021

Electronic Products
Garden City, NY 11530

Interface Age
P. O. Box 1234
Cerritos, CA 90701

Kilobaud
Peterborough, NH 03458

Microcomputer Digest
2589 Scott Blvd.
Santa Clara, CA 95050

Mini-Micro Systems
5 Kane Industrial Drive
Hudson, MA 01749

ON-LINE
24695 Santa Cruz Hwy.
Los Gatos, CA 95030

Personal Computing
1050 Commonwealth Ave.
Boston, MA 02215

Personal Computing World
62A Westbourne Grove
London W2, ENGLAND

Physician's Microcomputer
   Report
Box 6483
Lawrenceville, NJ 08648

Popular Electronics
One Park Ave.
New York, NY 10016

Radio Electronics
200 Park Ave. S.
New York, NY 10003

Recreational Computing
Box E
Menlo Park, CA 94025

Recreational Programming
Box 2571
Kalamazoo, MI 49003

SCCS Interface
P. O. Box 5429
Santa Monica, CA 90405

Small Business Computers
   Magazine
33 Watchung Plaza
Montclair, NJ 07042

Small Computer Systems
   Journal
P. O. Box 6733
Concord, CA 94524

Small Systems World
50 East Green Street
Pasadena, CA 91101

Small Systems World
53 West Jackson Blvd.
Chicago, IL 60604

Softside
P. O. Box 68
Milford, NH 03055

TRS-80 Computing
Box 158
San Luis Rey, CA 92068

TRS-80 Monthly Newsletter
Box 149RB
New City, NY 10956

TRS-80 Users Group Newsletter
629 Dixie Lane
South Daytona, FL 32019

The Intelligent Machines
   Journal
111 La Honda Rd.
Woodside, CA 94062

Word Processing World
Geyer-Allister Publications
51 Madison Ave.
New York, NY 10010

C MAGAZINE ARTICLE WRITING AIDS

Flesch, Rudolf, *The Art of Readable Writing*, Harper & Row.

Flesch, Rudolf, *Look It Up*, Harper & Row.

Hays, Robert, *Principles of Technical Writing*, Addison-Wesley.

Lewis, Norman, *The New Roget's Thesaurus in Dictionary Form*, Garden City Books, Garden City, NY.

Sipple, Charles J. and David Kiss, *Microcomputer Dictionary and Guide*, Matrix Publishers (dilithium Press).

Webster's New World Dictionary of the American Language, Prentice-Hall.

D SAMPLE SOFTWARE LICENSE AGREEMENT

The Center for the Study of the Future agrees to grant, and the customer agrees to accept on the following terms and conditions, nontransferable and nonexclusive license to use MAILOUT.

Terms

The agreement is in effect from the date of receipt of MAILOUT and shall remain in force until terminated by the customer or by the Center for the Study of the Future. The Center for the Study of the Future may terminate this license if the customer fails to comply with any of the terms and conditions of this agreement.

License

Each program license granted under this agreement authorizes the customer to use MAILOUT in any machine-readable form on any single computer system. A separate agreement is required for each computer system. This agreement may not be transferred, sublicensed or otherwise released for use on another system.

Permission to Copy or Modify Program

Under this agreement the customer may not copy this program or documentation except for use on his own system. No more than five copies of the manual or five copies of the program may be created for the customer's use. All must be clearly marked with the copyright notice. Proper records must be maintained of each of these copies, and each shall remain the property of the Center for the Study of the Future. The program may be modified for the user's specific application, but the copyright notice still must be included unless specific agreement is made with the Center for the Study of the Future.

Security

The customer agrees not to provide or make available the MAILOUT program to anyone except the purchaser or the Center. The customer will remain liable for any unauthorized use or copying.

Discontinuance

Within one month after the date of discontinuance of any license under this agreement, the customer will furnish the Center for the Study of the Future written notice that, to the best of his effort, all copies in whole or part and the original have been destroyed or returned to the Center for the Study of the Future. The Center for the Study of the Future will reimburse the customer for any media returned for which he has previously paid the Center.

Disclaimer

The Center for the Study of the Future makes no warranties with respect to the licensed program. The program is free of errors, to the best of the Center's ability. The Center will also provide the customer with all program updates for a period of one year from the date of purchase.

Limitation of Liability

The foregoing warranty is in lieu of all other warranties, expressed or implied, including but not limited to the implied warranties of merchantability and fitness for a particular purpose. In no event will the Center for the Study of the Future be liable for consequental damages even if the Center for the Study of the Future has been advised of the possibilities of such damage.

E   BOOK PUBLISHERS

Addison-Wesley Publishing Co., Inc.
Reading, MA 01867

Wm. C. Brown Company, Publishers
2460 Kerper Blvd.
Dubuque, IA, 52001

Marcel Dekker, Inc.
270 Madison Avenue
New York, NY 10016

dilithium Press
30 N.W. 23rd Place
Portland, OR 97210

Hayden Book Co., Inc.
50 Essex Street
Rochelle Park, NJ 07662

MacMillan, Inc.
866 3rd Avenue
New York, NY 10022

Matrix Publishers, Inc.
30 N.W. 23rd Place
Portland, OR 97210

McGraw Hill
1221 Avenue of the Americas
New York, NY 10020

Adam Osborne and Assoc.
(see McGraw-Hill)

Prentice-Hall, Inc.
Englewood Cliffs, NJ 07632

Howard W. Sams, Inc.
4300 W. 62ne Street
Indianapolis, IN 46268

TAB BOOKS Inc.
Blue Ridge Summit, PA 17214

F   BIBLIOGRAPHY

How to Package and Market Your Own Software Product, Datasearch, Suite 108, 730 Waukegan Road, Deerfield, IL 60015, $28.

Kirk, John, *Incorporating Your Business*, TPR Pub. Co., 321 Harwood Building, Scarsdale, NY, 1976, $12.95.

McQuown, Judith H., *Inc. Yourself*, MacMillan Pub. Co., Inc., NY, 1977, $8.95.

Nelson, Leslie, *How to Start Your Own Systems House*, Essex Publishing Co., 285 Bloomfield Avenue, Caldwell, NJ 07006, 1977, $24.85.

Nicholas, Ted, *How to Form Your Own Corporation Without a Lawyer for Under $50.00*, Enterprise Publishing Co., 1300 Market Street, Wilmington, DE 19801, 1975, $9.95.

The Shoestring, Start-at-Home, Computer Business Handbook, Datasearch, Inc., Suite 108, 730 Waukegan Road, Deerfield, IL 60015, 1977.

(We also suggest the books sold by the Entrepreneur Press, 468 Robert Road, Vacaville, CA 95688.)

G REFERENCES FOR SERVICE BUREAU OPERATIONS

Bernard, Dan, *Charging for Computer Services: Principles and Guidelines*, New York: PBI Books (384 Fifth Avenue, New York, NY, 10018), $10.

Although this is primarily written for large systems, some basic concepts are given that are valuable.

Dial, O. E., "Golfcap," *Personal Computing*, Vol. 1, No. 4 (July/August 1977).

Includes software to calculate golf handicap.

Fritz, Kenneth, "A Balanced Portfolio of Moneymaking Ideas," *Personal Computing*, Vol. 2, No. 1 (January 1978).

Gates, Reginald, "This is the House That Less Built," *Personal Computing*, Vol. 2, No. 2 (February 1978).

Estimating and scheduling service.

Gilroy, Henry, "Happy Holidays," *Personal Computing*, Vol. 1, No. 5, (September/October 1977).

Making income with games and puzzles (some FORTRAN software).

Hughes, Elizabeth, "What Should You Charge for Computer Services?" *Personal Computing*, Vol. 2, No. 1 (January 1978).

Norris, Glen, "Lemonade Planning For Sale," *Personal Computing*, Vol. 1, No. 2 (March/April 1977).

Includes software for cost projections.

Winkless, III, Nels, "Lemonade Computer Service Company," *Personal Computing*, Vol. 1, No. 1 (January/February 1977).

Service bureau computing for farmers.

H SOFTWARE DISTRIBUTORS

For cassette-based software:
dilithium Press
30 N. W. 23rd Place
Portland, OR 97210

Instant Software, Inc.
Peterborough, NH 03458

I SERVICE AGREEMENTS

COMPUTER SERVICE CORPORATION

Services:
*Repair, Contracts, Preventive Maintenance, Modification
Assembly, Installation, Consulting for the Laboratory*

Main Office: *621 North Street, Anycity, CA*

SERVICE AGREEMENT

CONTRACT TIME

Computer Service Corporation, hereinafter referred to as CSC, hereby agrees to provide _____, hereinafter referred to as Customer, with instrument service on any or all medical and bio-medical equipment for _____ hours based on a charge of $ _____ per hour. For these services to be performed by CSC, Customer agrees to pay the amount of $ _____ in advance.

The Contract, in its entirety, does not cover or include the cost of any and all parts sold by CSC to Customer. Nor does it cover or include any shipping, freight, or handling expenses involved in the sale or installation of such parts by CSC, except as may be covered by a manufacturer's warranty.

Travel expenses will be charged for at the rate of $ _____ per hour and $ _____ per mile, round trip, from CSC to the location specified by the customer.

For any service required after hours or on weekends, the mileage expense and travel time will be billed at one and one-half times the normal rate. There will be a two-hour minimum charge for repair labor for calls taken after hours or on weekends.

CSC agrees and expects to provide the above contracted service time within one year. However, any unused portion of this contract shall carry over into the following year, for a maximum of twelve months. CSC will provide a written report of any and all services rendered on all Periodic Maintenance Visits to Customer.

COMPUTER SERVICE CORPORATION

PREVENTIVE MAINTENANCE AGREEMENT

SERVICE—The subject of this agreement, preventive maintenance service, shall consist of cleaning, calibrating, adjusting the instruments and replacing therein, necessary components and parts.

During the term of this agreement, CSC will service the instruments at customer's installation, upon regular visits, scheduled at intervals of approximately _____ months, and will service the instruments upon additional visits, at the installation, if requested by the customer.

COMPONENT REPLACEMENT—CSC will not replace components or parts for which there is a charge, unless authorized by the customer. Charges for components or parts will be made at the current list prices.

SERVICE CHARGES—Customer agrees to pay CSC $6.00 per quarter hour of service time at the customer's premises, plus $15.00 per PM visit for travel from CSC's nearest service center to customer's premises, plus parts, plus any applicable taxes.

INSTRUMENTS—This agreement shall apply to the instruments and equipment described on the attached equipment listing. Other instruments may be added to the listing upon the mutual agreement of both parties.

WARRANTY—"CSC warrants that any parts or other components used in servicing customer's instruments shall be new and not defective in materials or workmanship. There are no other warranties, express, implied or statutory, made by CSC concerning the instruments as served by CSC under the terms of this agreement other than as immediately above set out."

TERMS; TERMINATION—The term of this agreement is one year from the date set forth below. Either party may terminate this agreement by written notice to the other; the termination shall be effective thirty (30) days after deposit of notice in the United States mail, postage prepaid, addressed to the other party at its last known principal place of business.

CUSTOMER _____   Computer Service Corporation
_____   621 North Street
_____   Anycity, CA
_____
                                  _____
                                  _____
CORP/PARTNERSHIP/PROPRIETORSHIP
BY_____   BY _____
TITLE _____   TITLE _____
PURCHASE ORDER NO.   SCIENTIFIC PRODUCTS NO.
_____   _____
DATE _____

INDEX